FIRE BENEATH THE CLOCK

Weaving Pentecost into the fabric
of Lancashire Christianity

FIRE BENEATH THE CLOCK

WILLIAM COUNSELL

New Life Publishing Co.

New Life Publishing Co.

Nottingham, England

First published in the UK, 2003

ISBN 0-9536100-1-2

Printed by Creative Print & Design, Middlesex.

Contents

Foreword

It has been both a privilege and a pleasure to have played a small part in the realisation of this study of Pentecostalism in central Lancashire in the first half of the 20th century. Donald Gee's *Wind and Flame*, Alfred Missen's *Sound of a Going* – and more recently William Kay's *Inside Story* – have all contributed to our understanding and knowledge of the Assemblies of God in Britain. But Bill Counsell's study, based on his successful M.Th. dissertation, adds another dimension.

Focussing, as the title suggests, on one area, Bill paints a vivid canvas and successfully blends Pentecostal history with the sometimes turbulent social history of the period. Characters like Fred Watson, Willie Hacking and Amy Entwistle spring to life; and tensions and problems are not glossed over but rather serve to hammer home the message that 'those who do not know their history are destined to repeat its mistakes'.

Commenting on the relatively modest impact that British Pentecostalism has had when compared with Scandinavia or the United States, Donald Gee pointed out that, as regards missionary work, the movement had an encouragingly stronger influence and impact than size and presence at home may suggest. Bill Counsell's account of missionary personnel, and enterprise from lively Pentecostal Assemblies like Preston and Blackburn, certainly bears this out.

I heartily recommend this colourful and well-documented account.

David Allen B.A., M.Th., Ph.D.
Dean and Senior Tutor, Mattersey Hall
– July 2003

About the Author

William (Bill) Counsell grew up in Blackburn under the ministry of Fred Watson and is married to Marion the niece of Alan Benson. He is a chartered surveyor and was a senior partner in private practice. He has pastored AoG churches in Grimsby and Leyland.

Bill is a director of three companies and has served on the National Executive Council and National Finance Committee of British Assemblies of God. He holds a Master of Theology degree from University of Wales, Bangor.

Preface

Around the turn of the 20th century there occurred within the Christian Church a well-documented outpouring of the Holy Spirit that, in the space of a few short years, was particularly manifested in locations throughout North America, Europe and Scandinavia. This Pentecostal phenomenon was to have ramifications in central Lancashire, largely as a result of a personal Pentecost being experienced by two devout Methodist businessmen: Thomas Myerscough of Preston and Frederick Watson of Blackburn.

Under the leadership of these two men, Pentecostal churches were established in the two towns. Within a few years there was within the area not only an expanding group of Pentecostal churches but also a Bible school and a missionary society, together with a small army of independent missionaries and pastors.

Whilst initially the emphasis was a local one, the Lancashire Pentecostals soon began to reach further afield. They played a substantial part in the growth of the Pentecostal testimony throughout Britain – including an important role in the formation of both British Assemblies of God and Elim Churches – and their missionary zeal took them around the world, in some cases leading to imprisonment and martyrdom. This book is an examination of that local phenomenon over the 50-year period from 1910 to 1960.

W. Counsell, August 2003

Apologia and Dedication

The author, a senior Pentecostal minister of long standing, is a native of Blackburn, and as a teenager was a member of the Blackburn Assembly in the days of Fred Watson. He is married to Marion, the niece of Alan Benson, a missionary to China. A substantial part of this account is based on personal recollections, records from the archives of some of the early pioneers, a variety of interviews and other selected reminiscences of family and friends, and it is dedicated to the memory of Thomas Myerscough and Frederick Watson without whom this story could not be narrated.

Note: Whilst the information presented in this book has been researched as thoroughly as practicable, much of it is nonetheless the recollections of 'yesteryear' and as such can only be as accurate as the memories of the sources from which it was obtained. If any details are found to be incorrect the author apologises unreservedly for such errors.

1

Lancashire in the Early 20th Century

In order for any examination of the local church in general or the Pentecostal outpouring in particular to be presented in a balanced context, it is essential that we first understand at least something of the background conditions which were prevalent, and the changes that were taking place, in the central Lancashire region around the time of the commencement of our narrative.

The industrial North of England includes an area of central Lancashire generally located around the lower reaches of the River Ribble and its tributaries. Although this region is an area of outstanding natural beauty, it also encompasses the two large post-industrial towns of Blackburn and Preston together with a host of smaller satellite towns and villages. The emerging history of these towns was fundamentally refocused around the middle of the 19th century, when the local rural weaving industry was overtaken by the industrial revolution. The latter soon gave rise to the numerous multi-storey cotton factories which sprang up, or so it seemed, almost everywhere. The unprecedented migration to the towns of central Lancashire that followed created an urban sprawl largely populated by a people with that very typical Northern resolve to survive under any circumstances. The two towns became the significant centres of population in the area.

Many economic and sociological changes had already taken place as the old century had drained away. By the turn of the new century, there were over 150 cotton mills in Blackburn alone, and by 1911 over half the labour force of the town was employed in textiles.[1] By that same year there were over

---

[1] Timmins, G., Blackburn, *A Pictorial History*, Phillimore & Co. Ltd., Chichester, 1993, p. 5.

60 cotton mills in Preston with textiles also accounting for about half of that town's workforce.[2]

The future of the two towns was full of promise, but there were still many problems and privations. Life was hard and, despite the prosperity manifest in many areas of life, the average working class family was facing a constant battle for basic survival.

Meanwhile, the enthronement of 'King Cotton' had spawned acres of back-to-back terraced houses, known as 'two-up-and-two-downs' (referring to the configuration of the accommodation), usually built in the immediate vicinity of a mill, which became the focus of life for the occupants. In the main, the housing was damp, unhygienic, unattractive and cramped. The only means of heating was open fires, but normally only the two rear rooms had fireplaces. Coal, that valuable and essential commodity, was often stored inside the house, with the inevitable result that food was not infrequently peppered with coal dust. Infant mortality rates were high.

With the very rare exception of a few philanthropic mill owners, there were virtually no provisions for relaxing or taking fresh air. Profits were high, but wages were low, and any infringement of the regulations by the workers was usually severely dealt with. The factories were dangerous places and injury and even death were not uncommon. In his account of a 13-year-old runaway, Burton records that the boy "suffered one of those accidents that were all too common among the unguarded machines of the mill."[3]

The annual 'Wakes Week' holiday to the nearby seaside – usually Blackpool – became for many, but by no means for all, a welcome break in an otherwise arduous life.

The two towns had grown beyond recognition in a short space of time and, by 1911, the population of Blackburn had

[2]   Timmins, G., Preston, *A Pictorial History*, Phillimore & Co. Ltd., Chichester, 1992, p. 5.

[3]   Burton, A., *The Rise and Fall of King Cotton*, British Broadcasting Corporation, London, 1984, p. 76.

increased sixfold compared with 1821.[4] The population of Preston had doubled in the period from 1837 to 1911.[5]

The prosperity of the cotton industry, and its many peripheral activities, continued apace. Indeed, it seemed to know no bounds and with the end of the Great War in 1918 it appeared to be more prosperous than ever. The post-war euphoria was to be short-lived however, and when the crash came in 1920 it was to shock the whole industry. But whilst to the prosperous mill owners it simply meant lost profits, to the workers it meant no food. "It didn't occur to anybody that Lancashire's world supremacy in cotton textile production had come to an end."[6] The ensuing years, which chronicle the demise of the cotton trade in Lancashire – "the contraction of textiles, in a town where almost every street had a cotton mill, dominated the inter-war years"[7] – also abound with stories of personal struggles with poverty, unemployment, sickness and sheer hopelessness.

But, throughout these difficult and turbulent years, the churches of the day played their part in the social life of the area and had their effect on the mood of the times. One well-known writer of social history, William Woodruff, a native of Blackburn, readily remembers how during a period of his life – when he found himself sympathising with a Communist agitator – he wondered why the workers did not revolt in his day as they had done almost a hundred years earlier.[8] Clearly there was some restraint, so it is interesting that he concludes that "perhaps religion helped. Strong Nonconformists and Roman Catholics don't sit well with Communism."[9]

Times were very hard, and Woodruff recalls how, as late as 1932, his own father could not come to terms with earning

---

4   Timmins, G., Blackburn, *A Pictorial History*, Phillimore & Co. Ltd., Chichester, 1993, p. 6.

5   Timmins, G., Preston, *A Pictorial History*, Phillimore & Co. Ltd., Chichester, 1992, p. 5.

6   Woodruff, W., *The Road to Nab End*, Abacus, London, 2002, p. 44.

7   Hunt, D., *A History of Preston*, Carnegie Publishing Ltd., Preston, 1992, p. 233.

8   *Preston Chronicle*, Preston Riots, Black Saturday, 13 August 1842.

9   Woodruff, op. cit., p. 388.

money breaking up looms. Just a short while before, he and men like him had been employed to keep those very looms in first-class condition.[10] Indeed, a hundred years before, men had been hung for smashing looms. Now they found themselves being paid to do it!

---

[10] Woodruff, W., *The Road to Nab End*, Abacus, London, 2002, p. 353.

2

Religious Conditions in the Early 20th Century

The turn of the 20th century was set to become a significant point in the life of the Church of Jesus Christ worldwide, but particularly that wing of the Church which embraced a fundamental interpretation of the Bible. This involved a personal experience of life-transforming salvation from sin – a basic teaching which crossed many denominational barriers in the Protestant and Nonconformist ranks of the day.

Historically, England had, under God, produced some great evangelical Christian leaders and reformers such as Wesley, Whitefield, Booth and Spurgeon. These men, with a host of others – each in their own day – had a profound effect on the impact of Christianity in society. And a number of these leaders had witnessed a limited amount of charismatic if not Pentecostal outpourings in their services at various times. A similar story could be told of men like Edwards, Finney, Moody and many others in North America.

The Church had come through some very significant experiences but, by and large, those sections of the Western Church which had continued in a fundamentalist tradition over the years had nevertheless tended to neglect the supernatural in their Bible teaching and practice. Large sections of the Church had adopted a 'cessationalist' approach. That is to contend that the biblically-recorded experiences of the operation of gifts of the Holy Spirit, miracles and healings, ceased with the end of the initial Apostolic Age and therefore had no place in the life of the contemporary Church.

Many Bible students of the work of the Holy Spirit – whether for or against – are aware that over the centuries the gifts and manifestations have always continued to be evident within the Church at various times and in sundry places.[11] These various outpourings which Pentecostals attribute to the sovereign work of the Holy Spirit have been sometimes small and sometimes quite large, often criticised and disputed, but always significant: "The Church is, above all, the earthly and temporal residence of the Holy Spirit."[12]

Around the turn of the 20th century, many Christians of different spiritual backgrounds and in widely scattered locations all across the world felt that something was missing from their spiritual experience. As they carefully studied the Scriptures they became increasingly aware that God had clearly promised something more than they were experiencing. It is either pure coincidence or highly significant that this seeking 'for more of God', and the subsequent spiritual awakening which followed it, both occurred simultaneously in many areas quite distant from one another – and not just in miles but often also in forms of worship. Pentecostalists believe that the numerous spiritual outpourings which occurred in a number of countries over a relatively short period of time are not only highly significant, but also a fulfilment of Bible prophecy such as that recorded in Joel 2:28 – "And afterwards, I will pour out my Spirit on all people."

It was on New Year's Day 1901, in Bethel Bible College in Topeka Kansas USA, after the students had been asked to examine and discuss Acts 2, "that Agnes Ozman received a tongues-attested baptism in the Spirit."[13] Not long afterwards, the Holy Spirit was poured out in an old warehouse building in Azusa Street in downtown Los Angeles in 1906.

The phenomenon was also witnessed in Britain in the chapels of the Welsh Valleys in 1904 and in an Anglican church at Wearmouth, Sunderland, in 1906. Similar events were occurring simultaneously in many other distant places, notably in Sweden, which was soon to boast the world's largest Pentecostal church of the time. In the recent work of Harvey Cox, which

---

[11] Gee, D., *The Pentecostal Movement*, Victory Press, London, 1941, p. 9.

[12] Allen, D., *The Unfailing Stream*, Tonbridge, Sovereign, 1994, p. 5.

[13] Allen, op. cit., p. 108.

is a very detailed examination of worldwide Pentecostalism, he concludes that from the Azusa Street outpouring "a spiritual fire roared forth which was to race around the world and touch hundreds of millions with its warmth and power."[14] This is a remarkable conclusion by a man who is not a Pentecostal himself!

Far from being welcomed by the established Church, the Pentecostal experience and those who embraced it were generally received with scepticism at the best and often downright denunciation at the worst. We shall see later that many of those leaders who received a personal Pentecost in the early 1900s were men of integrity, whose overriding desire was to take the new experience back into their historic churches to bring some new spiritual dimension. More often than not, however, the reaction they received was total rejection, not infrequently demanding recantation if they were to retain their existing links of fellowship.

Their rejection became a challenge, causing them to reconsider their strategy and bringing them ultimately, albeit with reluctance, to the place where they felt compelled to proceed to form their own initially independent Pentecostal churches.

It is significant to note that this initial rejection of Pentecostals was not a purely British phenomenon, but was evident in other places around the world. Following extensive research, Cox observes that "preachers and lay Christians who responded to the new message were often rejected and ridiculed, and had to start churches of their own."[15]

This renewal of spiritual experience seemed remote from Lancashire. Preston and Blackburn were typical of many northern towns of the period. Blackburn was largely Protestant whereas Preston was predominately Roman Catholic, indeed the name Preston is a derivation of 'Priest's Town'. The recent period of intense industrial growth had inevitably also seen many churches of various persuasions erected in the two towns as part of the developing architectural scene. And,

---

[14] Cox, H., *Fire from Heaven*, London, Cassell, 1996, p. 46.
[15] Cox, op. cit., p. 249.

among the more evangelical movements, the Methodists and the Salvation Army were well established in the communities, and each in their own way was doing a good work. The general mood, however, was to accept the presence of the Church rather than its persuasion. Whilst many of the churches of the day were quick to reject the new outpouring, the general public's attitude to the Church, and to any changes taking place within the Church, tended to be one of apathy rather than rebellion. Reflecting on his own attitude and perhaps that of many of his contemporaries, native of Blackburn, William Woodruff, readily declares in his book that his 'spirituality' was clearly dictated by hunger: "We sang anybody's hymns, provided tea and rock buns followed."[16]

---

[16]   Woodruff, W., *The Road to Nab End*, Abacus, London, 2002, p. 156.

3

Men with a Vision

The Pentecostal experience that burst forth in locations all across the Western World early in the 20th century was soon to have ramifications in the towns of central Lancashire.

Far away from Lancashire in the late 19th century, a young man who was a keen horseman and of farming stock was growing up in a small village in Teesdale. Frederick (Fred) Watson was born in 1882 and, like many of his contemporaries, he was expected to make a life in his native dales. He left school at twelve and was apprenticed to the village blacksmith for seven years. It certainly seemed that the rural way of life had attracted him, and that his life would be spent in the valleys of his fathers. However, other factors that were to prove crucial were already beginning to influence his life. His family were staunch members of the local Methodist Church and were keen for young Fred to follow in their Christian tradition.

At about the time of his 21st birthday, an itinerant evangelist was invited to hold a 'revival campaign' in the village church. Although the campaign services yielded negligible results and could certainly not be described as a success, a plan by some of the church officers to close the meetings was rejected. So the services continued as originally planned and, on the last night of the services, the prayers of young Fred's mother were answered when he responded to the preaching of the evangelist by accepting Jesus Christ as his Saviour. Shortly afterwards, he left the village to take up a junior post in insurance in the northern town of Whitehaven.

When country boy Fred arrived in the town in 1903, he could so easily have been swallowed up in the life of the town and the challenges of his post, but his new faith had already become a major force in his life and he quickly linked himself with the local YMCA. There, he became involved in organising some very successful evangelistic outreaches in the area, a sure sign that his faith was taking root in his life and thinking. Whilst in Whitehaven he married a young lady from his native Teesdale, and also began to climb the ladder of promotion within his company.

The promotion he was offered inevitably led him away from Whitehaven, and, after service in the Great War, when Fred returned to civilian life to rejoin his company, it was as a branch superintendent in Blackburn. He arrived in Blackburn in around 1918, at just about the time when the cotton industry's prosperity bubble of the previous century was about to burst.

The Fred Watson who arrived in Blackburn as the senior businessman had, by that time, come a long way from his northern village roots. Were it not for his readiness to talk freely about his youth, it would certainly have been hard to imagine that he had ever trained as a blacksmith. He was a well-built, upstanding man of some presence, always immaculate and invariably sporting a bow tie, a characteristic which was to be copied by others in later years, notably Lawrence Livesey. He appeared austere and somewhat remote, but had a soft heart, strangely coupled with some strong theological views on which he could be totally inflexible. Members of his family related that he had a rather impish sense of humour, which was known only to those closest to him.

Apart from his business success there was a spiritual fire burning within him and, having settled in Blackburn, he soon aligned himself with the YMCA and the Methodist Church in the town. He became a well-respected figure and a prominent member of a band of local preachers among whom his influence was considerable.

But he was hungry for a deeper Christian life. During his earlier military service he had heard of the baptism of the Holy Spirit, so he and a fellow officer of a similar mind had spent much off-duty time together, walking in the woodland near to their camp, seeking this deeper spiritual experience.

Although neither of them had come into the experience of receiving the baptism and speaking in tongues, the deep inner yearning he had felt in those days not only remained with him but also grew even stronger over time.

With his strong evangelistic fervour, Fred was instrumental in obtaining permission for a series of outreach meetings in the churches of his local Methodist Circuit, and during these meetings a number of young people in the Mosley Street Church became born-again Christians.

Feeling unfulfilled, and with that deep spiritual hunger still unsatisfied, he drew around himself one or two of the younger local preachers, along with a number of the new Christian converts from the Mosley Street services, and they too began to share his desire for closer fellowship and a deeper spiritual experience. One of the younger local preachers, William (Willie) Hacking, who was training for the Methodist ministry, was not sympathetic towards the group, but their simple faith caused him to re-examine his own liberal views and he too began to seek a deeper spiritual life.

It was not long before the group began to hear reports of various series of meetings being convened by similar groups, where the Holy Spirit was manifestly in operation. At Easter 1919, Fred, along with a friend, attended some such meetings in Bradford.[17] These meetings, which were overtly Pentecostal, left a deep impression on him, not least in the area of divine healing. He brought back home to his sick wife a handkerchief that had been prayed over in the Bradford services, and she was remarkably healed of goitre. It was at about this time that he informed his local group that he had also heard of some similar Pentecostal meetings being held at a location much nearer home.

A number of years earlier, just a few miles away in Preston, another professional man, Thomas Myerscough – a middle-aged estate agent with a Methodist background who had been deeply influenced by the reports of the recent Pentecostal outpourings in Sunderland and found his own

---

[17]   Hacking, W., *Frederick Watson*, R. Seed & Sons, Preston, 1953, p. 13.

heart yearning for a deeper Christian life – heard of some similar meetings being held in the home of a Thomas Mogridge in nearby Lytham. Mogridge himself had experienced the baptism in the Holy Spirit whilst on a visit to Sunderland in 1906.

Myerscough, a well respected, albeit austere, bearded man of some bearing, had already gathered around him a small group of people who were seeking, as he was, a richer spiritual experience. He arranged for some of their number to visit the Lytham meeting early in 1908 and they were deeply impressed by the experience. On their return to Preston they spent a number of days carefully studying the Scriptures together and became convinced that what they had witnessed was the sovereignty of God in restoring the gifts of the Holy Spirit to his Church.

Myerscough attended the 1909 Whitsuntide Pentecostal Convention in Sunderland and there received his own personal experience of Pentecost and spoke in tongues.[18] By 1911 the Preston group were meeting together on a regular basis, a number of them seeking, and receiving, their personal Pentecostal baptism.

With Myerscough's many contacts as an estate agent, the members of the fledgling assembly were soon located in their own rented base – a large upper room over Starkie's Wire Shop in Lancaster Road in the centre of Preston. This was an address that was destined over the ensuing years to become sacred in the memories of many families, not only in Preston but also in many a far-flung land. Donald Gee, a well-known Pentecostal writer, later records that "As a result a Pentecostal centre was established in Preston that has been second to none, perhaps in the world."[19]

The setting up of this group had not been planned or intended. Thomas Myerscough, despite his deep spiritual yearnings had no desire whatsoever to encourage anyone to leave their historic denominations. Indeed, he was opposed to

---

[18]   Acts 2:4.

[19]   Gee, D., *The Pentecostal Movement*, Victory Press, London, 1941, p. 59.

the idea. In practice, however, the seemingly unquenchable zeal of his followers and the cold reception they received in their churches as heralds of Pentecost made the ideal unattainable – and so the break became inevitable.

The decision to form their own fellowship had not been taken lightly and they neither presumed nor desired to call themselves a 'church' nor to acquire any type of ecclesiastical building. The groups, once they were formed, simply became known as Pentecostal Missions and were more than content to be located in whatever accommodation their limited budget would enable them to acquire.

By 1919, the Preston Pentecostal Mission, which Myerscough had started, was well established and had been holding regular meetings for some time. Myerscough himself, already a well-respected businessman, soon also became widely recognised as a very able Bible expositor. It is a mark of the respect in which he was held at the time that the official Bible School of the recently established Pentecostal Missionary Union was, during this period, relocated to Preston from the South of England and placed under his care.

The Bible school was located in the rooms over Starkie's Wire Shop. The 'student body' of those early days included men such as George Jeffreys and WFP (Willie) Burton who were destined to leave their own mark in Pentecostal circles in Britain and beyond. In these formative years for Pentecostalism, some dramatic events were beginning to unfold. The ultimate telling of these would become almost legendary for future generations, among them being the missionary call of Burton and Salter and their departure for Central Africa, which is dealt with later in this book.

It was at around this period that the Preston meetings came to the notice of Fred Watson, and within a very short time both he and the members of his little band were regular visitors at the weekly Monday night Bible Study meetings in that large upper room over Starkie's Wire Shop. So began a strong relationship between the two men – which was to last until the death of Thomas Myerscough in 1932 at the age of 74

– and the formation of a link between two embryonic Pentecostal groups who, through mutual support, have had a marked effect on many lives both at home and overseas.

Willie Hacking – one of the original band of Methodist local preachers linked with Fred Watson – who had now joined the group, later described a specific event that took place on one of their earlier visits to the Preston meeting.[20] Having heard that Smith Wigglesworth – a noted healing evangelist from Bradford – would be the speaker, the group took along with them a woman who was chronically ill and could only move around her home by using the furniture as a means of support. They soon found that the sheer logistics of getting her onto the train, across Preston and up the 45 steps to the meeting room were far more arduous than they had initially imagined!

They were tired, the meeting was long, and they became preoccupied with ensuring that they caught the last train. Smith Wigglesworth's frequent practice was to pray for sick people at the end of his sermon, but the timing of the prayer time varied meeting by meeting, depending on the length of the sermon. As the service progressed, the visitors became increasingly apprehensive when the sermon was not finished, and it was approaching the time of that last train to Blackburn.

However, their fears were unfounded. Wigglesworth interrupted his sermon to pray for the woman and, afterwards, she was so wonderfully healed that she ran in front of the group all the way to Preston station. The resulting change in the home was nothing short of dramatic. Within a short while her alcoholic husband was so impressed and challenged by his wife's healing that he was born again too. His life was transformed and in due course he joined the group and became the first treasurer of the Blackburn Mission.

The Preston meetings were demonstrably Pentecostal with fervent preaching, the regular operation of spiritual gifts – including tongues, interpretations, prophecy and healings – and constant open challenge to the adherents to develop

---

[20] Hacking, W., *Frederick Watson*, R. Seed & Sons, Preston, 1953, pp. 23 - 25.

greater zeal and devotion. The services were regularly well attended and were always followed with eager anticipation.

The visitors from Blackburn were continuing to attend their own churches as Fred Watson insisted repeatedly that they were not to break their ties with the established churches.

A number of members of the group were still active on the Methodist local preachers' circuit plan. Over the ensuing weeks, however, the desire for stronger ties of fellowship continued to grow until, under increasing pressure from the group, Fred relented and agreed to hold Friday night Bible studies in his Blackburn home. Whatever his intentions were at the outset, he had almost by default become the leader of a body of people who were now single-minded in their aim of establishing vibrant Pentecostalism in their own hometown.

Typical of the period, he was always known to his followers as 'Mr' or 'Brother' Watson, but was nevertheless deeply respected by them. The new fellowships had already adopted the use of the titles 'Brother' and 'Sister' when addressing one another, and by mutual consent these titles were often applied to their leaders, to demonstrate that "they were all one in Christ Jesus". Over time, the use of these titles also inferred acceptance into the group – which deemed the use of any form of clerical attire or title by their leaders to be unacceptable. This view later became the norm for British Pentecostals generally.

At one of the regular Friday night meetings, after a lengthy discussion about how to make a greater impact on the town, a decision was taken to commence regular open-air services on Sunday nights at eight o'clock and they began to consider alternative locations. To their surprise, Fred Watson related an incident that had taken place on a Sunday night some twelve months earlier, soon after his arrival in Blackburn. While standing alone under the tower supporting the market hall clock in the centre of the town, and watching the crowd passing by, he had felt a compelling compassion for his fellow man. Taking off his hat, and "with tears streaming down his face, had claimed that ground for God."[21]

The matter was resolved – they would meet under that clock! Thus began a tradition that lasted for over 25 years. And, by its location, the meeting place was protected from the northern weather and proved to be an ideal weekly meeting place – come summer or winter. The formal creation of a Blackburn Pentecostal Assembly was inevitable, and many of its future members were to 'find new life in Christ' under that clock.

It was not long before more converts began joining the band and numbers grew too great for the regular Friday night house meeting. Larger premises became a necessity and so, after some searching, the minister's vestry in the Montague Street Congregational Church was leased for the growing Friday night Bible studies. Willie Hacking recorded that the word 'vestry' was something of a misnomer, as the large room would easily accommodate up to sixty people.

The break with their traditional roots was now complete, and a regular Sunday morning service was commenced in the YMCA hall in Limbrick, Blackburn. But there was no indoor Sunday evening meeting because the market place was their church. The Pentecostal Mission in Blackburn was now established.

---

21   Hacking, W., *Frederick Watson*, R. Seed & Sons, Preston, 1953, p. 19.

4

The Early Years

The Preston Pentecostal Mission had been started in 1911 and around 1920 the Blackburn Mission was also established. The Preston Mission, as already noted, was located in a large upper room over Starkie's Wire Shop and accessed by 45 steps.

In Blackburn, the members of the newly formed Mission began to search for a place of their own and ultimately homed in on an upper room in Cort Street. It is interesting to note that the Bible records that the first Pentecostal blessing fell on an upper room in Jerusalem,[22] and these two fledgling Pentecostal Missions were also found in upper rooms.

Starkie's Wire Shop was situated in the town centre on Lancaster Road, a rather respectable location on a main thoroughfare in Preston. Cort Street on the other hand was in a tumble-down area of downtown Blackburn, just behind Victoria Street on the fringe of the central shopping area of the town. These early days in Cort Street were not easy. Stories abound of leaking roofs, buckets and umbrellas being in great demand during services on wet days, a landlord whose interest in the property was limited to collecting the rent, and many other difficulties that would have destroyed a less resolute congregation. They, like the converts in Hebrews,[23] might well have returned from whence they came – in this case the relatively comfortable and well-organised Methodist churches. But a fire had been kindled which would not easily be extinguished. Indeed, it is evident on reflection that they came to regard their worst experiences, such as spiritual rejection and poor standards of accommodation, as blessings rather than handicaps.

Bearing in mind Fred Watson's business background and

---

[22] Acts 1:13.
[23] Hebrews 11:15.

standing in the town, it is quite remarkable that he not only drew this group together but continued to lead them, many of whom were from a totally different social stratum from the one to which he belonged. It is interesting to note that whilst both Fred Watson and Thomas Myerscough were professional men, their adherents generally were not. In Blackburn they were largely from a working-class background whilst the Preston group tended to be predominately lower-middle-class.

Willie Hacking clearly illustrated this difference in social strata by relating[24] a particular occasion when Fred Watson arranged for a week-long series of evangelistic outreach meetings to be held adjacent to the site of their regular weekly open-air services at the Market Hall. For the location of the services, he booked a rather opulent suite of rooms over a furrier's shop, complete with a liveried commissionaire on the door and at a cost of £40 – an arrangement with which he no doubt felt most comfortable. The members, however, generally felt totally overawed both by the selected venue and the cost, and, surprisingly, they challenged Watson's judgement. However, when he in turn contended that the money was well spent, the arrangements he had made were approved.

At the event, Teddy Hodgson from the Preston group was the invited speaker but the meetings produced only one convert, a young Blackburn weaver named Jim Fowler. Though the general lack of response may have seemed disappointing at the time, Jim eventually became a missionary to Africa. So who can measure the final result of the venture?

By the early 1920s the upper room in Lancaster Road was becoming crowded, so it was usual for the congregation to overflow onto the steps leading up to the room. And it was also not unusual for the meetings to continue well into the evening – so those who had travelled to Preston from nearby towns by train or bus often found that they had to leave before the meeting ended if they were to catch their transport home. But leaving early was not an attractive option, so these out-of-town visitors often missed the last bus or train and

---

[24] Tape-recorded interview with W. Hacking, May 2001.

stayed overnight with a local family. Then, early the next morning, they caught the first train and went directly to their place of work.

These decisions to stay over were spontaneous and usually involved some *ad hoc* arrangement such as sleeping on the floor. Indeed, on many such occasions the meeting itself often 'spilled over' into the home and ran on into the early hours. On one typical evening Hubert Entwisle from Blackburn was reported to have received the baptism of the Holy Spirit during a late night meeting at his Preston 'lodgings'.[25]

Whilst the growing attendance was doubtless a blessing, the resulting congestion in the upper room over Starkie's shop was an increasing problem. More spacious accommodation became essential, and once again Myerscough's position as an estate agent was advantageous in the ensuing search for a suitable building. It was not long before he located six small cottages due for demolition in a street just behind Lancaster Road, only a short distance from their existing address. The cottages – which backed the site of the bus station – were purchased and demolished by the church in 1923, and then a fine, purpose-built hall was erected, no mean achievement for the group!

Much of the work was executed by the members themselves, and four of the founder members became trustees. At last, the Preston group of the Central Lancashire Pentecostals had a permanent home of their own with what were extensive facilities for the period – including a baptismal tank for water baptism services by total immersion.

It is noteworthy that within a very short period the new hall was debt free. Glad Tidings Hall in Cheetham Street was destined to hold a very special place in the lives and memories of a veritable host of Pentecostals over the ensuing years. Existing in the heyday of public transport, the location immediately adjacent to the bus station was ideal.

By 1925 some 300 people had been baptised in water at Cheetham Street. In 1926 another milestone was passed when Doris and Clarence Stobbart were married in the hall. Theirs

---

25 Tape-recorded interview with Mrs L. Norcross, May 2002.

was the first wedding to be conducted by the Lancashire Pentecostals in their own building. Later, within a few years, the hall was extended and the spacious new main hall held perhaps around three hundred people, and it was not uncommon to see all the seats occupied and a number of people having to remain standing throughout the services on Sundays.

Sometime in the early 1920s, perhaps around the same time that the Preston folks were building their new hall, Fred Watson sprung a surprise one Sunday morning. He took a few of his supporters to inspect a 'back street' hall further down Cort Street that had become available for rent. It was an old Church Army Hall – a rather sad, old, wood-and-corrugated iron structure – in need of attention and decoration. But it could seat some 250 people, it was a ground floor situation, much more spacious than the old upper room, and it was available at a rent of about £1 per week. So the challenge was accepted and within a short while the new hall was operational. But even so, they "possessed nothing that was at all elaborate."[26] It was from this simple unpretentious hall that the group was to send out pastors and missionaries to proclaim the Gospel around Britain and the world.

These early 20th century Lancashire Pentecostals – unlike their denominational contemporaries – placed little or no importance on presenting to society any form of architectural identity. They saw spiritual emphasis as their sole and divine mandate. Indeed, when their own church properties were eventually purchased, many of them considered normal maintenance expenditure to be a waste of money that could be better used in the support of foreign missionaries. These decisions may seem unwise to some people today, but these pioneers of Pentecostalism were certainly sincere and single minded. It has to be said that the numerical growth in those years was at least some vindication of the pioneer spirit which they exuded.

All adherents of the two fellowships were encouraged to seek a personal Pentecost and to operate the gifts of the Spirit. There was also a general sense of freedom in the services that

---

[26] Hacking, W., *Frederick Watson*, R. Seed & Sons, Preston, 1953, p. 30.

encouraged congregational participation by the reading of a verse of a hymn that specifically expressed some personal sentiment, or a word of testimony about some recent spiritual experience of the speaker. The meetings had an element of spiritual spontaneity rather than being totally controlled by the leaders.

It is a matter of record that Fred Watson was perhaps the less strict of the two leaders. On one occasion, whilst in discussion with Donald Gee, he admitted to "suffering fools gladly" in preference to the possibility of limiting the genuine. But at the same time he hastened to acknowledge that when at times zeal abounded at the expense of wisdom, there was need for the leadership to exercise control and give direction.

These were typical 'teething troubles' of a new move of the Holy Spirit in the nation. And, despite the inherent weaknesses, there were times of great blessing and many lives were changed dramatically.

5

The Rising Tide

The Pentecostals, who had hitherto grown largely through invitations to gatherings by word of mouth, were also intent on taking their message into their hometowns by public declaration. The weekly open-air meetings under the market hall clock became regular features of the Blackburn scene and were in parallel with the similar weekly meetings held in Preston on the central open market.

The onlookers, although often numerous, were not always sympathetic or supportive, and hecklers were not uncommon. But people were coming, standing and listening, and that was the declared aim of the group. The open-air services, once established, afforded regular opportunities for the more zealous members to step forward and become practised at public speaking. Clearly, some of the attempts had very embarrassing moments, but skills were undoubtedly developed – and sometimes by the most unlikely characters. It is not surprising therefore that, over time, a veritable army of capable preachers, pastors and missionaries was raised up from among these ordinary folk – many of whom honed basic evangelistic skills at these open-air services. The two young churches continued to grow.

Both Myerscough and Watson were very aware that zeal and ability, whilst commendable, were not the sole requirements for the budding leaders. Sound Bible teaching and 'anointing' were essential. To early Pentecostals 'anointing' was that God-given touch which turned a mere speaker into a incisive preacher – whose message impressed the hearers and spoke directly into their inner being, challenging them to respond. Both of the leaders were themselves already well established as Bible expositors and teachers and they therefore embarked on providing systematic training by regular

Bible studies in their respective fellowships. Usually there were three Bible studies a week, sometimes lasting as long as two hours, and the members attending were encouraged to keep notes both for future reference and to assist them in preparing their own sermons. Invariably, these Bible studies were well attended.

The fledgling Pentecostal Missionary Union had for its part already demonstrated complete confidence in Myerscough, by relocating its Bible School to Preston under his care. It is a matter of record that he amply discharged this responsibility over the years, and a roll-call of those people who studied under Myerscough – many of whom became central figures in Pentecostal circles in subsequent years – makes an impressive list.

It was increasingly evident that both the members and the new converts needed a wider forum for regular encouragement and challenge in addition to the Bible teaching and training associated with the weekly church programme.

The two leaders themselves had both been deeply influenced in their search for a personal Pentecost by attending specially convened 'convention' meetings. We have already noted that Myerscough attended a Whitsuntide gathering in Sunderland in 1909 and that Watson had attended a similar Easter event at Bradford in 1919. So, not surprisingly, it is a matter of history that both of these visits proved to be pivotal in the life of the respective fellowships.

Conventions were occasions when a number of Pentecostal leaders came together at selected locations, usually where some form of Pentecostal 'outpouring' had already been experienced, and preached to quite large gatherings over two or three days – often but not always over a bank holiday weekend. These convention weekends were always times of spiritual refreshing and rededication, and they were often frequented by numbers of non-Pentecostals who were either seeking a deeper personal spiritual experience, or who had come merely to see the phenomenon of Pentecost for themselves at first hand.

The gatherings also gave the many embryonic local groups a sense of belonging to something much greater as they met with other Pentecostals from much further afield. So it is not surprising that Myerscough, believing that there was a strong case for setting up a local convention, arranged the first Preston Easter Convention in 1920. The Preston Conventions were destined to become a major annual feature in British Pentecostal circles for over 80 years until they finally succumbed to changing times. As might have been expected, Fred Watson was regularly one of the invited preachers at a number of the early Easter Conventions.

Although the early Pentecostals implicitly believed that the success of any spiritual venture could only occur as a sovereign act of God, they also knew that God uses men.[27] It was clear therefore from the outset that the choice of speakers and convenor for the convention would be of some importance in both its initial impact and ultimate recognition.

The Bradford Convention that Fred Watson attended in 1919 had been started some time earlier by Smith Wigglesworth,[28] who was also to be instrumental in the establishing of the Preston Convention. Wigglesworth was a former Bradford plumber who had been transformed remarkably by his personal Pentecostal experience and had become an itinerant evangelist with a well-attested and miraculous healing ministry with world-wide acclaim. His involvement was both solicited and appreciated by his friend, Myerscough, so Wigglesworth convened almost all of the Annual Easter Convention Services at Preston from their formation in 1920 until his death in 1948.

Myerscough, meanwhile, generally led the singing on his portable Bilhorn organ. There can be no doubt that the regular presence of such a revered man as Wigglesworth had a positive influence on the extent of the support – from both speakers and congregations – which the services enjoyed.

---

27 2 Peter 1:21.
28 Whittaker, C., *Seven Pentecostal Pioneers*, Marshall Morgan & Scott, Basingstoke, 1983, p. 28.

Undoubtedly, he played a major role in the success of the Preston Conventions.

The conventions normally ran from Good Friday through to Easter Monday with three meetings – all well attended – each day. Two or three national and sometimes international Pentecostal figures were invited to the convention each year as speakers, and normally at least two of them would address each meeting. Additional 'fringe' meetings were arranged during the weekend for those seeking a personal baptism in the Holy Spirit and also for those who were candidates for water baptism by immersion. These people were usually new converts.

It soon became a tradition for cups of tea to be made available between the services, and visitors from out of town often spent the whole day on the premises. Local pastors and visiting speakers usually enjoyed a full meal prepared by the hosting ladies, and members of the host church opened their homes to visitors for the duration of the convention. Many lifelong friendships were established in this way. The conventions developed into important social gatherings for Pentecostals generally and, over the years, it was not uncommon to find married couples whose first meeting had been at a convention weekend.

The Easter Monday afternoon and evening services were set apart for great missionary meetings, when new missionaries who were preparing to embark for the mission field would share their vision and returning missionaries would relate their experiences on the field. The gatherings ended with a challenge to the young people present to consider offering themselves for missionary service.

These missionary services always included a special offering and it is a tribute to the zeal of the Pentecostals that on Easter Monday 1927 an offering of over £200 was received – a substantial sum in those days! The money raised was, of course, used to support missionaries and was not appropriated by the local church.

As the convention evolved, some of the early missionaries

such as Salter and Burton were welcomed back home to Preston, not only as returning missionaries but also as principal convention speakers in their own right.

For the first few years, the convention was held in the hall over Starkie's Wire Shop until 1923, and then it was moved to the new building at Cheetham Street. But by 1927 the growing congregations were too large for their own hall and the services were transferred to the more spacious Saul Street Methodist Church. Then in 1941, as attendance figures continued to increase, the convention was moved again – to Lancaster Road Congregational Church, and then on to Cannon Street Congregational Church in 1948. The missionary day services on Easter Monday 1949 recorded a capacity congregation of 1,200 and an offering of £2,013. And by 1950 the Good Friday services – which had grown substantially – were convened at the Public Halls in Lune Street, where the congregations could be measured in thousands.

The mixed venue arrangement continued into the 1960s and the Easter Monday missionary offerings remained a significant feature of the convention. In the 1950s these offerings often exceeded £2,000 and at their peak they actually topped £4,000.[29]

During the '50s offerings were preceded by moving appeals from ex-missionary Mrs Alice Salter, the daughter of Smith Wigglesworth. Alice developed a distinct style that won her a special place in the affections of the congregation. It is interesting to note that whilst Wigglesworth saw many dramatic healings, his own daughter remained permanently deaf.

Sometime in the late 1920s the first New Year Pentecostal Convention was convened at Blackburn, following a similar pattern to the already well-established Preston Convention. The Blackburn services ran from New Year's Eve and through New Year's Day and included the nearest Saturday and Sunday. There was always a sense of disappointment when New Year's Day fell on either Saturday or Sunday and so inevitably resulted in the convention being shortened.

---

[29]   Tape-recorded interview with T. Bilsborough, June 2002.

It is not surprising that a feature of the convention was a late-night New Year's Eve open-air service under the market hall clock and that, from time to time, New Year revellers became converts.

For a number of years the convention was held in the hall in Cort Street. Later, as attendance grew, the missionary day services were held in the large Congregational Church at the top of Montague Street. When Zion Chapel, a redundant Methodist Church located lower down Montague Street, was purchased by the fellowship in 1938, the meetings were transferred to their own church building.

The Blackburn Convention was never as well attended as the Preston Convention, New Year's Day was not widely recognised as a public holiday, and Smith Wigglesworth was not involved to the same degree. The convention did, nevertheless, soon gain recognition nationally and the Montague Street church often had a capacity congregation of around 450 people at many of the convention services.

The format of the services generally followed that at Preston, with two or three national figures as invited speakers who addressed the main convention services, and culminated in two great missionary rallies on New Year's Day. The existence of the two conventions strengthened the bond already established between the two fellowships.

But while considering the meetings' similarities, it is significant to note that, from their inception and throughout the whole of the period we are considering, neither of the convention programmes included any services specifically designated for young people or children.

Meanwhile, as many of the smaller churches in the area became established, they too arranged their own local annual conventions, and it was not long before there were one or two Pentecostal conventions taking place almost every month in central Lancashire alone.

The two fellowships continued to grow stronger, but in the late 1920s the Blackburn group discovered that history was about to repeat itself when they learned that a similar event to the one that had brought Watson to the town some years before now heralded his departure. He informed the church that he had received the offer of another promotion by his company, this time to an appointment in Liverpool, which was to take effect early in 1930. It was a major blow to the fellowship.

Watson, meanwhile, discussed his impending business transfer from Blackburn with Willie Hacking, who had already moved away into pastoral ministry, and suggested that he should visit Blackburn to consider returning to the church and taking some part in the pastoral oversight after Watson moved to Liverpool.

The two men agreed that Willie would attend the coming New Year services to discuss the matter further, but when Willie arrived in time for the Convention he found that Watson, in typical style, had pre-empted his decision and publicly announced to the fellowship that he was coming back to assist in the leadership of the church.[30]

Although Willie returned to Blackburn and fulfilled a pastoral role in the church for almost eight years, Fred Watson did not actually relinquish his overall control of the church over those years. Being a member of that very select band of people who owned a motor car in the early thirties, he drove over from Liverpool to Blackburn almost every Sunday morning, conducted Sunday afternoon Bible studies, and often also came over for the Tuesday evening Bible studies. His regular visits continued until 1938, when another transfer by his company – this time to the Chorley area – enabled him to live in Blackburn again, whereupon he resumed the full pastoral responsibilities. He was to fulfil the pastoral role at Blackburn for the rest of his life.

---

[30]   Hacking, W., *Frederick Watson*, R. Seed & Sons, Preston, 1953, p. 31.

6

Developing Churches

The growth of the churches soon necessitated that the leaders, either by design or by default, were required to give attention to the development of forms of government, styles of leadership and orders of services. In formulating their operational procedures they wilfully made little reference to their past associations. The Pentecostal zeal that motivated them and that had resulted in the break with their historic Christian denominations gave pre-eminence to what they saw as the spiritual thrust of their venture, and they resisted anything from their past which for them had come to be regarded as worldly.

Once the break with their past was implemented, they also saw it as complete, and rejected much that, with hindsight, might have been recognised as worth retaining to their advantage. Whilst both leaders were very strong on doctrine – in later years both men had clauses written into the deeds of their church property that prevented the appointment of a pastor who did not believe in the eternal security of the believer – they were opposed to implementing any system of formal membership for their followers. They deemed that everything must be rejected unless it had a spiritual dimension. But despite the tendency to inflexibility, they did not rule on every issue. For example, young men were left to make their own decision when the time came for national service – whether to enlist or to make a formal objection to undertaking military service. There were also some interesting differences between the two fellowships: whilst in Blackburn young men were strongly advised by the eldership not to attend university, this was not the case in Preston.

Their basis of faith was fundamental, evangelical and Pentecostal, based on a literal interpretation of Scripture. They were

Puritanical in their way of life. To them, salvation from sin included deliverance from *inter alia*, sex outside of marriage, gambling, smoking, dancing and cinema-going – all of which were seen as 'worldly'. Bazaars, jumble sales, concerts and the like were all seen as having contributed to the perceived decadence of the churches that they had left and were inadmissible as part of any church programme. So all events and activities had to be spiritual to be acceptable. Fundraising activities of any sort were simply banned.

Finance was raised by teaching the biblical principles of tithes and offerings – that is that one tenth of income belonged to God and was to be given to the church, and offerings were gifts made to the church after tithes had been given. Although these principles were regularly taught, they were not rigidly enforced. The actual decision whether or not to tithe was left to the individual and was not monitored by the church, but people generally responded to the teaching. Throughout the early years in Blackburn no collections were taken up during the services, which ensured that visitors or newcomers were not embarrassed. The regular worshippers simply placed all their tithes and offerings in a box at the rear of the church. It became the practice for any money not expended within a given financial year to be distributed to their missionaries, which, in the case of Preston, often took the form of a donation to the Congo Evangelistic Mission (CEM). Fred Watson regularly reminded his treasurer that it was his considered opinion that for the church to have any money in the bank was "a sin".

The coming together of a number of independent Pentecostal churches resulting in the formation of Assemblies of God in 1924 – described later in this book – also included the drawing up of "a carefully worded Statement of Fundamental Truths"[31] which became the doctrinal basis of faith and fellowship. This was not only for the original group of churches, it also became an entry requirement imposed on any other churches subsequently seeking to associate themselves with the Assemblies of God. Whilst the adoption of

---

[31]   Gee, D., *The Pentecostal Movement*, Victory Press, London, 1941, p. 143.

these fundamental truths was clearly beneficial to the leaders of the Blackburn and Preston Assemblies, at a time when one or two strange doctrines were emerging in some areas, it is noteworthy that the absence of any form of local membership meant that the leaders did not require the individual members of their congregations formally to adopt these fundamentals.

Their zeal was all consuming, and, as a result, there was in some respects an unfortunate overreaction to the traditions of the churches that they had left. A number of practices which were harmless and perhaps even beneficial were seen as decadent. Youth meetings, women's meetings, annual prizes or parties for the children in Sunday school were all frowned upon. The elders meeting at Preston in June 1932 recorded in their minutes that "no women's meeting be allowed". Indeed, any practice that was deemed to have had any part in the perceived decadence of the established churches was totally discarded. Interestingly, this practice, which the late great Bible teacher Professor F F Bruce referred to as *via negativa*, was not as uncommon as the Pentecostals might have thought. The practice had occurred before when the originators of a new Christian tradition, having noted what was customarily done in the churches which they had left, felt that their safest course was to do something different.[32]

The very special position that the two leaders held in the new fellowships as founding fathers meant that they commanded a considerable amount of respect. There is no record that either leader ever faced a challenge to their leadership. In each of the churches that deep respect, coupled with the lack of any contemporary precedent for Pentecostal church government, resulted in the creation of a spiritual autocracy. Benign and benevolent it may have been, but an autocracy nonetheless.

As founding fathers both Watson and Myerscough were deeply respected by their followers, but each was well aware that future leaders of either of the assemblies at Preston or Blackburn would be highly unlikely to enjoy the same level of

---

32   Bruce, F. F., *In Retrospect*, Marshall Pickering, London, 1993, p. 7.

respect which they had been able to command. It is interesting
to note that, whilst they both ultimately appointed a board of
elders to oversee the future of the church and to secure the
succession in due course, there is no record that either of
them ever submitted themselves to their local board. And,
apart from the period when Watson was posted to Liverpool
and Hacking assisted him in the pastoral duties, both men
continued in their rather autocratic leadership roles until
within a few weeks of the time of their deaths.

The methods that the two men adopted for the appointment
of elders were very different. Myerscough personally selected
twelve men from the Preston congregation to form the initial
board, using the biblical record of selection of disciples by
Jesus as a model. Watson, however, announced his decision
to embark on the formation of a board to the assembled
Blackburn church and simply invited any men in the congregation who felt the call of God to office to 'come and take a seat
at the front'. It is a tribute to Watson's leadership qualities and
his implicit faith in God's sovereignty that such a system could
possibly operate effectively. It is virtually inconceivable to even
imagine that any pastor would dare to take such a step today!

The strict observance of Sunday as a special day was
fundamental to early Pentecostals, and was one of the issues
on which Watson wrote to the local papers on a number of
occasions. The production of a magazine by the Congo
Evangelistic Mission in the 1920s posed a major problem,
because the thought of making any form of purchase on
Sundays was totally unacceptable, and there was no question
of making exceptions for Christian literature. For many years
the Blackburn church resolved the matter by purchasing
copies of every issue of the 'Congo Report' and making them
available to all members of the congregation free of charge.
When Assemblies of God introduced 'Redemption Tidings'
some time later, that too was provided on free issue by the
church.

7

Outside Links

The turn of events that had been experienced by Myerscough and Watson in their respective towns was soon also occurring in various other locations throughout the British Isles. Fellowships were being formed in other places and coming together in local groups. It was only a matter of time before a much wider fellowship than that which was shared by the two men would evolve.

Their early links with Wigglesworth widened their spiritual horizons. He had already established a wide reputation as a thoroughly Pentecostal minister with numerous demands on his time; and the inevitable contacts which resulted from his many travels, together with the growing reputation of the Easter Conventions following his personal involvement, brought them into contact with other men of like mind.

A typical example was a Pentecostal pioneer J N Parr, a Manchester businessman, who had established a thriving Pentecostal church in the Longsight area of the city. Other churches in the north-west were becoming well-established and links were being formed with the leaders of a number of independent Pentecostal churches throughout Britain, some as far away as South Wales.

The Pentecostal church was growing apace, but rapid growth was also producing divisions and factions that were threatening the stability and reputation of the Pentecostal testimony. Gee records the existence of a "twofold menace... of erroneous doctrine and practice."[33]

Early in the 1920s there came together a group of men who were anxious to secure and preserve the Pentecostal testimony in Great Britain. There was no doubt in their minds that some sort of grouping needed to be established, but they were

---

[33] Gee, D., *The Pentecostal Movement*, Victory Press, London, 1941, p. 140.

resolutely opposed to creating a new denomination. Among their number were Myerscough, Watson and Parr. It is not the purpose of this book to report the progress of their endeavour. Suffice it to record that, after much deliberation over an extended period of time, the Assemblies of God in Great Britain and Ireland was finally brought into being in May 1924 as a fellowship of autonomous independent churches, and an Executive Council of seven men was appointed to oversee the new fellowship. The seven men selected included the three from Lancashire, with Parr elected as the Chairman. History records that although Myerscough, as the younger man, deferred to Parr, he nonetheless played an important role in the negotiations. It is evident that Myerscough was held in high esteem by his contemporaries: "It seemed as if almost the only independent leader remaining at that time with sufficient personal prestige to launch a movement for organised fellowship with any prospect of success was Thomas Myerscough of Preston."[34] Both Watson and Myerscough continued to serve on the Executive Council throughout a number of the early years of the British Assemblies of God.

Blackburn and Preston were among the first churches in Britain to become Assemblies of God Churches, and it is of interest that one of the early ministerial certificates of recognition issued by the new fellowship dated October 1925 was granted to W Hacking of Blackburn.

The Preston church, which had demonstrated an early interest in overseas missions, also played an important role in facilitating the work of the Congo Evangelistic Mission as it emerged from the initial missionary enterprise started by Willie Burton and Jimmy Salter in 1915, which is covered in more detail in a later chapter. When the two pioneers first ventured into Congo, they were initially accredited by the Pentecostal Mission of Johannesburg, South Africa, but in November 1919 Burton wrote to Salter recording that he had resigned as the Congo Branch of that Mission. Regular reports had been submitted by Burton back to the Preston church (via Johannesburg) from the start.

---

[34]	Gee, D., *The Pentecostal Movement*, Victory Press, London, 1941, p. 142.

Early in 1920 the Congo Evangelistic Mission (CEM) came into being and its official home-based headquarters was established in Myerscough's own estate agency offices in Lawson Street, Preston. Regular reports continued to be dispatched from the field but they were sent direct to the Preston office and, not surprisingly, in due course the title 'Congo Report' became the name adopted by the official magazine. The 'Congo Report', first produced in September 1921, initially with a limited circulation, was established some two years later in July 1923, when it was published for sale priced at 2d – less than 1p per copy at today's prices!

Throughout many of its earlier years, the printing and distribution of the report was in the hands of H Webster of Elterwater near Ambleside. Despite all his other responsibilities, Myerscough ably served as the CEM secretary until his death in 1932, whereupon the office was relocated to the home of his son, Philip, at Broughton, near Preston, and was run by Philip and Myerscough's sister for some eight years.

In 1940, the office was again relocated. This time to the Penwortham home of J Jolly who served as the secretary and produced the Report from 1940 until his death in 1949. On the death of Jolly, the work was again divided when John Parker, who had recently returned from Jamaica, accepted the appointment as secretary,[35] but only on the express under-standing that some other person would be responsible for producing and distributing the Congo Report.

Tom and Alice Billsborough took responsibility for the production of the magazine. The staff changes of 1949 afforded an opportunity to establish a totally independent office and a suitable property at 355 Blackpool Road, Preston, was duly inspected, acquired and adapted by the CEM as its permanent headquarters. Parker served until 1970, when the Billsboroughs were appointed to assume overall responsibility. The offices have remained at the same address up to the present time.

In the 1920s and '30s, three young men from one Welsh

---

[35] Tape-recorded interview with T. Billsborough, June 2002.

family had a marked effect on the spiritual thermometer of Britain. Stephen, George and Edward Jeffreys came from a mining background in the valleys of South Wales. After initial periods of fruitful ministry in their immediate locality, all three men conducted major spiritual revival and divine healing crusades in towns across Britain – with memorable results.

Years earlier, George had attended Myerscough's Bible school at Preston, but it was Edward, the youngest of the three, whose crusades in Preston and Blackburn during 1931 were to prove unforgettable for the region. Edward had been filled with the Holy Spirit as a lad of ten and, years later, he recorded his Pentecostal experience: "I received a definite baptism of the Holy Spirit, and I began to speak in tongues as the Spirit gave me utterance."[36]

After a very successful series of meetings in Blackpool in 1931, Edward moved over to Preston and commenced a crusade in September of that year in the Majestic Skating Rink. On the first night the rink was only half full, but soon capacity crowds of around 3,000 people were attending nightly. Then the daily attendance increased to around 5,000, whereupon he moved to the Public Hall. Over 9,000 converts were recorded during the period of the crusade, with a further 800 conversions resulting from a short, five-day visit to nearby Leyland. Attendance was so good that, every night, hundreds of people were unable to get into the crowded services!

On 24th November 1931, Edward moved on to Blackburn and commenced services in the King George's Hall on Northgate. The local paper reported of the first night, "In spite of the unfavourable weather nearly 3,000 people attended last night."[37] Within a few days the hall was filled to capacity almost every night and 3,000 conversions were reported during the first ten days of services.[38]

---

[36] *The Bethel Full Gospel Messenger*, Volume 5, Number 12, December 1931, p. 187.

[37] *Northern Daily Telegraph*, 24 November 1931.

[38] *The Bethel Full Gospel Messenger*, Volume 5, Number 12, December 1931, p. 200.

One outstanding Blackburn healing[39] was that of a blind man who eventually accompanied Edward on a number of his crusades, and finally settled in the Cort Street church with his entire family. Within a short space of time a number of people joined the Pentecostal congregations, not only at Cheetham Street and Cort Street, but also at some of the branch churches following the Jeffreys' successful series of crusades in the area.

---

[39] *The Bethel Pictorial Guide*, 1928 – 1938, p. 16.

8

Reaching Out

As the work continued to grow, word of the meetings began to spread to surrounding areas, and people seeking a deeper spiritual life came into the towns to the services, reflecting the journeys made by Watson and Myerscough just a few years before. The regular congregations of the two churches soon included individuals or families who travelled in from a number of surrounding towns and villages.

Working hours were long and travelling was difficult, and although the determination and resolve of the Pentecostals was more than enough to overcome the obstacles, the leaders saw a unique opportunity not only to establish branch churches in those areas where a group already existed but also to enable the people concerned more effectively to evangelise their own district. The 'mother churches' acquired rooms in selected towns, and soon branch churches were springing up in a number of strategic locations, including among others Rawtenstall, Accrington and Bamber Bridge.

The system employed to monitor these young churches was interesting. For example, the churches established from Blackburn maintained the link through their leader, who was usually a personal appointee of Fred Watson, selected by him from among his own congregation. Each leader, once appointed, was required to continue to attend the mid-week Bible study at Blackburn in addition to fulfilling his new charge. It was not uncommon during the 1930s to see as many as eight or nine pastors of branch churches in attendance at the Tuesday night Bible studies. The continuance of their tenure of office was entirely at Watson's discretion. They were encouraged to take notes of Watson's sermons that, in turn, formed the basis of their own ministry that week and ensured sound teaching.

But not all Blackburn branch ministries were pastored by people from the mother church. Just a few miles away over the moors, young Isabel Campbell and her mother heard of the move of the Holy Spirit in Blackburn and visited Cort Street in the late 1920s. They returned to their local church in Haslingden, where they shared their new Pentecostal experience with two young mill boys, Fred Ramsbottam and Maurice Hugo. Both were zealous new converts with a deep spiritual hunger, and soon they too were regular visitors to Blackburn and received their personal Pentecost. The three excited young people returned home full of spiritual 'fire' and anticipation, but when they eagerly recounted their experiences to the pastor of the local Holiness Church, expecting his support, they were shattered when he firmly denounced their new experience and declared that "this teaching you have expoused (sic) is a dangerous falsehood."[40] He demanded that they must either recant or leave the church.

They were devastated, but, unable to deny their personal Pentecostal baptism, felt that they were left with no option but to leave. Undaunted, the three of them, the two boys and Isabel, preached and testified of their faith in the town and, before long, they were able to hire a hall in which to commence Pentecostal services. Both Watson and Myerscough gave their personal support and attended the opening service.

Within a short while there was a thriving fellowship in the town and soon young Fred Ramsbottam was able to leave his job at the local mill to pastor the church. Not long afterwards, Isabel and Fred were married. Far from recanting and settling down, Fred, Isabel and Maurice were destined to take the Gospel not just to Haslingden and the local area but also to the heart of Africa.

Meanwhile, a few miles from Blackburn, in the opposite direction to Haslingden, a young Leyland farmer, Edmund Cross, and two Methodist friends made a number of visits to the Preston Cheetham Street Mission in the mid 1930s, and soon all three were filled with the Holy Spirit. They were

---

40 Ramsbottam, F., *African Plenty*, Marshall Pickering, Basingstoke, 1987, p.20.

deeply challenged by the Cheetham Street meetings and, following a number of very encouraging discussions with Fred Watson, a house fellowship was started in Leyland in 1938. The local group began to grow and later that year a small purpose-built hall was erected in Hastings Road, and Edmund Cross became their first pastor. He led the church until 1956, when the church appointed its first salaried minister.

The two churches positively encouraged a spirit of evangelism typical of Pentecostals and, at the suggestion of Willie Hacking, the Blackburn church purchased a marquee that was used in the 1930s. Willie set it up in various towns and villages throughout Lancashire from time to time and held series of services – sometimes lasting a few days, sometimes for a few weeks.

On one occasion, the marquee was used for services in the centre of Great Harwood. Willie relates that, during the period of preparation, he felt the need to publicise the proposed meetings in the town beforehand and then bravely confronted Watson, who at that time was firmly opposed to any form of advertising. Willie confessed to being rather surprised that approval was finally given for the printing and distribution of handbills announcing the services, particularly as the leaflets he proposed to use included his photograph.[41]

A number of people who attended those services were deeply challenged and found new life in Christ, resulting in the establishment of a very healthy Pentecostal church in the town at the conclusion of the services in the tent.

One of the early converts in Great Harwood was William (Bill) Hartley, who later married Laura Wilson from Preston. Bill, who pastored churches in the south of England, also exercised a well-authenticated itinerant ministry in divine healing, and ministered extensively in North America over a number of years. Lawrence and Margaret Livesey, who later became missionaries to South India, were the first pastors of the Great Harwood Church.

The marquee was used in various locations, and members

---

[41]   Tape-recorded interview with W. Hacking, May 2001.

of the Blackburn group took the opportunity to be involved in convening and preaching in the services, which not only resulted in an effective spiritual outreach but also became another practical training ground for potential ministers and missionaries.

The Preston church started their branch works primarily by holding open-air meetings in nearby towns such as Coppull and Chorley. In the mid 1920s, J Jolly – a member of staff at the County Offices in Preston – being one of the few members of the Cheetham Street fellowship to own a car at that time, dedicated his vehicle to evangelism. He regularly took a carload of people to the outlying towns and villages, including Coppull and Chorley and even as far as Wigan, to hold open-air Gospel services. As people responded, various local groups were formed and he subsequently became the founder of the Wigan Assembly.[42]

A healthy church was also established at Bamber Bridge on the outskirts of Preston, and was pastored for many years by John Shepherd who had been converted at Cheetham Street.

Sunday 20th March 1932 marked the end of the initial era in Pentecostalism in Lancashire with the passing of Thomas Myerscough at the age of 74.[43] Smith Wigglesworth conducted the funeral of his friend four days later and Fred Watson took part in the service.

The respect which Myerscough commanded was fittingly marked by the attendance of mourners from many parts of England and Scotland. It is typical of the man that, despite a full commercial life, he had simultaneously held office as treasurer and secretary of the Congo Evangelistic Mission, founder member of the Presbytery of Assemblies of God, and pastor of the thriving congregation at Glad Tidings Hall in Cheetham Street. He had also for many years been responsible for the Pentecostal Missionary Union Bible School, and he had remained active in the leadership of the church until within one month of his death.

---

[42]   Tape-recorded interview with Mrs. D. Coates, daughter of J. Jolly, May 2002.

[43]   *Redemption Tidings*, Volume 8, No. 4, April 1932.

Shortly prior to his death, Myerscough, although not having formally trained a successor, recognised the need for future effective leadership, and indicated his preferred successor chosen from among the men of the assembly. He had selected Richard Coates, a member of the board of elders. In a final tribute to Myerscough, the appointment of Coates was readily endorsed by his fellow elders and he was to pastor the assembly for 20 years.

It is a strange twist to this record of Lancashire Pentecostal history that Myerscough chose as his successor a man who was not yet baptised in the Holy Spirit. Coates was 48 years of age when he became the pastor in 1932. He was a much more private man than Myerscough, a man of a quiet and indeed somewhat introvert nature, and a very able Bible expositor. He, like Myerscough before him, had a full-time occupation and his appointment to the pastorate was a non-stipendiary one.

Unlike Myerscough, who worked locally, the posts Coates held as an engineer at Elswick Hospital and later at Wrightington Hospital – some 15 miles south of Preston – made it difficult for him to attend all the services. So there were long periods during his tenure of office when Coates was only able to be present at the services on Sundays. But, by standing arrangement, the weeknight services were frequently conducted by the other elders, which inevitably tended to increase their authority. So, over the ensuing years, there were times when the elders at Preston exercised their powers unilaterally – sometimes at the expense of the incumbent pastor.

It is a matter of record that, for many years, the two assemblies appointed successive pastors from their own ranks. The first 'outsider' was not appointed until the early 1960s, when Lawrence Livesey left Blackburn to return to South India.

As the numbers attending the Cort Street services continued to grow, Fred Watson began to search the town for larger and more substantial premises in which to house the congregation. In the late 1930s he discovered that the rather large and imposing Congregational church at the top of Montague Street was for sale for £1,000. This was the very building in which the Pentecostals hired a vestry for their first public services. But while Fred hesitated in his deliberations, the building was acquired by the Bethel Fellowship who had established a church in the town following the Jeffreys crusades. Shortly afterwards, Zion Chapel – a smaller building with some 450 seats lower down the same street – became available in 1938 for just £450, leading Watson to believe that his earlier failure to acquire the larger building had actually been a blessing in disguise.

This building also had strong links with their past. It was ironic for Watson and Hacking, who had earlier left the Methodist Church, that they and their followers were now able to purchase the Central Church of Primitive Methodism in Blackburn,[44] where they had both preached years before – "The exiles returned as owners".[45] An old photograph, which the Methodists left behind, was allowed to continue to hang in the vestry at Zion Chapel for many years; it was a picture of a group of Methodist Local Preachers – including Watson and Hacking.

The original name of the church building was retained, and Zion Chapel was destined to be the spiritual home of the Blackburn Assembly for the next 30 years. But the tenure of the Bethel church in the larger building at the top of the steep incline lasted only a few years, ending when a private loan was recalled, necessitating the sale of the building. Had Watson bought the larger building he would have obtained a loan from the same source.

Watson's effective use of a design feature of Zion Chapel gives a typical insight into his character. He expected young men to preach their first sermon on reaching 16 years of age, and young preachers need guidance on how to face a congregation. At the rear of the church was a large stained glass

44 Hacking, W., *Frederick Watson*, R. Seed & Sons, Preston, 1953, p. 38.
45 Gee, D., *These Men I Knew*, Assemblies of God Publishing House, Nottingham, 1980, p. 88.

window depicting John Chapter 10 and showing the shepherd
returning with the lost lamb. Watson's instruction to young
preachers was to look at the window and keep their eyes "on
the lamb" to avoid distraction. In giving this advice to the
young men he was also establishing the sound spiritual princi-
ple that their eyes must always be on another lamb – Jesus, the
lamb of God.

9

Problems and Difficulties

The embryonic Lancashire Pentecostal churches were not free from problems. Although they had, in the main, emerged from the churches of established denominations, they discarded many of the practices and characteristics of those churches. At that relatively early stage there was minimal help available in the way of practical guidelines from their Pentecostal contemporaries, thus requiring them to establish in a short space of time tenets of faith, systems of government, orders of services, modes of worship and rules for living. It is a tribute to the two leaders and a mark of the respect in which they were held, that despite the absence of any real points of reference they were able to oversee effectively the creation and development of stable churches, and yet retain the Pentecostal essence of spontaneity and freedom of expression in worship.

It is both interesting and perhaps even providential that whilst, in the main, the early British Pentecostal believers tended to be working-class or lower-middle-class, many of their founding leaders, including Myerscough and Watson, were business or professional men whose higher station in life secured for them a modicum of respect. In the absence of any form of authoritative clergy it is this early respect for leaders that doubtless played a part in procuring the initial stability and growth of British Pentecostalism. The fact that both Myerscough and Watson continued in office up to shortly before their deaths was paradoxically both a weakness and a strength. In the later years of their lives there were some limited areas of resistance to both men that would have been inconceivable in the earlier years of their leadership of the respective fellowships.

The very nature of Pentecostalism, which encouraged personal experience and expression, inevitably brought its own problems with certain individuals who took advantage of the freedom that the leaders allowed. Fred Watson was a realist. On one occasion, whilst discussing a particularly troublesome church member with Willie Hacking, he reflected that "If the Church were perfect, he [God] would require no shepherd, and we might be looking for a job in politics."[46]

Paradoxically, one of the strong points of Pentecostalism became one of its weaknesses. Many of the new converts shared their faith with those with whom they were acquainted, with the result that on occasions members of the same street or place of work were also converted along with members of their own families. Sometimes whole families joined a local fellowship. Whilst the conversion of family and friends is undoubtedly a blessing, it could also present problems. As churches became established and were given their independence, some of the smaller churches found that a large proportion of the congregation was from one family. In an autonomous system of church government this situation was a potential problem for a small church. Over time, in some instances, the predominant family took control of the fellowship to the detriment of the local testimony. Such situations placed a question mark over the wisdom of autonomy, particularly in the case of small churches.

Another paradox existed as a result of the devotion that many early Pentecostals demonstrated by their deep involvement in the life of the church. Whilst the high level of commitment was undoubtedly a crucial factor in the growth that the churches enjoyed, this same commitment often resulted in young children being regularly taken to services that frequently continued long into the evening. A number of these children, who did not come to share their parents' zeal, felt robbed of their family life and rebelled against the system, rather than the faith, with the not infrequent result that, as they grew, they were lost to the church.

There were periods when certain doctrinal differences potentially threatened the survival of an effective Pentecostal

---

[46] Hacking, W., *Frederick Watson*, R. Seed & Sons, Preston, 1953, p. 60.

testimony – both nationally and locally – which placed an added burden on the leaders particularly, although not exclusively, in the period leading up to the formation of Assemblies of God in 1924. Donald Gee wisely observed that "The baptism in the Holy Spirit renders no believer immune from the possibility of falling into error."[47]

In the early days of the Pentecostal outpourings, the meetings that were vibrant and spontaneous would often run late into the evening or even into the early hours. Unfortunately, over time, this developed a distinct mindset among some leaders that short services were a sure sign of returning to the denominational decadence that had been left behind. There emerged in some quarters an unwritten policy that meetings that continued until late evening must by definition be good meetings. This irrational view, coupled with the apparent inability of some leaders to close meetings at a reasonable time, became a real problem in the Pentecostal services of the late 1950s – a problem aggravated by the fact that the services themselves were tending to be much more stereotyped in practice than the earlier Pentecostal gatherings had been.

The internal problems which the emerging Pentecostals faced were compounded by the attitude of other Christians. The initial rejection which Pentecostals suffered at the hands of the established churches was not abated over time. Indeed, a few churches in the two towns persisted in denouncing Pentecostalism as demonic, whilst some actually banned their members from attending Pentecostal services or associating with Pentecostals generally. Christians down the centuries had had to face being rejected by the world, but early 20th century Pentecostals had to face being rejected by other Christians.

The fast-occurring world events also brought problems to the Pentecostal missionary endeavour. The 20 years from 1940 to 1960 saw tremendous changes. The gross disruption caused by the 1939-1945 war in Europe and the Far East made

---

[47] Gee, D., *The Pentecostal Movement*, Victory Press, London, 1941, p. 139.

communication and travelling between the mission field and the homeland both difficult and dangerous.

This period was followed by Communist incursions into Tibet and China – effectively banning all European missionaries from those lands. And the uprisings in Congo following independence in the early 1960s permanently changed the scene in Central Africa for missionary work, initially causing all Western missionaries to be withdrawn – with the ultimate martyrdom of Mr E (Teddy) Hodgson and Elton Knauf by the rebels when the missionaries returned to attend to the welfare of suffering believers on the mission field.

Around the same time, the eruption of some internal problems and misunderstandings in the churches in South India necessitated the return of the Liveseys from retirement. They were extremely well respected by all the Indian churches concerned, and were able to bring about reconciliation. The Liveseys were to visit India on at least ten more occasions, and were spared long enough to see a great spiritual harvest in southern India.

It would not be unreasonable to suggest that the cumulative effect of such varied events in a relatively short period of time seemed to indicate that the timing and intensity of the pre-1940 missionary outreach by the early Pentecostals had been divinely led.

10

Expanding Overseas

The fervent zeal that had been a hallmark of the early days of the two churches was not limited to passion for Lancashire – or even England. Soon, these ordinary Lancashire lads and lasses, who in the normal course of events might never have travelled much further than Blackpool for a 'Wakes Week', began to feel compelled to take the Gospel around the world. This overwhelming sense of compulsion, which defied all natural logic and human reasoning, was born of a deep desire that the Gospel of Jesus Christ, which had so revolutionised their own lives, should be shared with the whole world as directed in the New Testament.[48] This intense desire they referred to as the 'call of God' on their lives.

Their leaders, and Thomas Myerscough in particular, always poured 'cold water' on these aspirations, not with any intention to discourage but in order to ensure that they were absolutely genuine. Fred Ramsbottam, whilst relating his personal experiences during interviews with Myerscough, observes that "in the Mission's view more was needed to make a missionary than simple zeal."[49]

In the early days of Preston Assembly, Thomas Myerscough's Bible classes had been attended by Willie Burton, a young engineer employed at Dick Kerr's factory in Strand Road, Preston. Indeed, within a year or two, young Burton was assisting Myerscough with the lecturing. By 1910's standards Willie Burton was from a very privileged background – his father had been the Commodore of the Cunard [shipping] Line, and his godly parents had a profound effect on his life. After taking an engineering course in the south of England, he came to work at Dick Kerr's engineering factory

---

48 Mark 16:15.
49 Ramsbottam, F., *African Plenty*, Marshall Pickering, Basingstoke, 1987, p.30.

in Preston and, whilst there, continued to study at Liverpool and soon qualified as an electrical engineer.

When working for his company on a contract in Batley in Yorkshire, he committed his life to Christ on 3rd August 1905 and he records that "the change was immediate and dramatic".[50] This decision was to have spiritual repercussions far greater than could ever possibly have been imagined. He was 19 years of age.

One of the students entrusted to Burton was a young cobbler living with his Aunt in Preston, James (Jimmy) Salter, who had begun to attend the upper room over Starkie's shop. He was just 18 years old. Despite their very different backgrounds, Willie Burton and Jimmy Salter formed a friendship which was to last a lifetime and was to be the basis of a unique venture into central Africa that was to affect literally thousands of lives in the subsequent years.

Together, they developed a 'burden' for Africa and decided to set out as missionaries. After spending some time in South Africa they arrived in the former Belgian Congo in 1915. Thus commenced what was destined under God to become a great missionary enterprise – known as the Congo Evangelistic Mission. Its head office, initially based in Thomas Myerscough's Estate Agency Office in Lawson Street, is still based in Preston to this day.

It is significant to note that Burton, having realised that many missionary societies had "been handicapped by men in their armchairs directing operations of which they knew nothing", insisted from the start that the operational running of the mission would be in the hands of the staff on the field, and he ensured that this policy was maintained over the years.

The two men, Burton and Salter, set out from Preston and arrived in South Africa, where they shared their vision around the churches as they prepared for their journey into the interior. There was a lot of interest in their venture and

50   Whittaker, C., *Seven Pentecostal Pioneers*, Marshall Morgan & Scott, Basingstoke, 1983, p. 149.

they were joined by two other would-be pioneers, Armstrong and Blakeney, who shared their zeal for a missionary enterprise focused on central Africa.

The group of four finally set out for Congo after extensive discussions with a Mr Johnstone, also originally from Preston, who, having just returned from a recent visit to the Belgian Congo, advised them to make their base at a place he identified as Mwanza Hill, a natural vantage point in a relatively thickly populated area.

The journey was arduous in the extreme. The railway ended at Kambove, where they spent a month with some American Methodist missionaries from whom they learned much about life in the interior. Their trek included travelling up the great Congo River, but after reaching the riverbank it took two days before they were able to join the river steamer, which lay stranded on a sandbank – where it remained for a further eleven days after their arrival. Living conditions on the old, iron boat marooned under the blazing African sun were unbearable. Within a short time, the oldest member of the party, 'Daddy' Armstrong, who had been suffering from a fever for some days before reaching the steamer, died and was buried beside the Congo River. Blakeney, who was suffering from malaria, had to be carried back to the boat from his friend's graveside.

Burton, the leader of the group, was approached by some British military officers – fellow passengers with considerable experience in Africa – who, after seeing the dire physical condition of the three remaining missionaries, strongly recommended that they abandon the journey and return to England before it was too late. But after much heart searching, despite all the odds that seemed stacked against continuing the journey, Burton felt a deep reassurance of the call of God and rejected their advice. The three remaining pioneers battled on – facing more crises along the way.

For the larger part of the journey Salter suffered from acute malaria and had to be carried by the porters in a make-shift hammock. They finally arrived at their recommended destination, Mwanza Hill, in September 1915.

In many aspects their arrival was somewhat of an anti-climax. All three men were weak and extremely unwell, and the initial difficulties they faced were potentially over-whelming. So much so that, within a month of their arrival, Blakeney succumbed to the pressure and "dropped a veritable bombshell on the two younger men"[51] by announcing his decision to quit and promptly left to return to civilisation.

Burton and Salter were alone again – but they had arrived! The two men persevered against tremendous odds and their zeal was duly rewarded. Burton later recorded that, by 1932, over 300 assemblies were meeting and "over 16,000 natives (sic) had confessed their faith in baptism."[52] It must be noted that Burton's statistics were limited to those who were baptised, and doubtless many other Congolese were associated with the work but had not been baptised at that time.

It is not surprising that in the early days Burton and Salter made a number of basic policy decisions. One of these was that, as the Congo of 1915 was clearly no place for Western women, their endeavour would be strictly a 'men only' operation. Once settled on the field, however, Burton found that African cultural attitudes relating to immorality had to be considered. As Europeans, he and Salter faced grave misunderstanding with regard to sexual implications if they even talked to women and children, let alone attempted to share the Gospel with them.

As soon as they had finished building huts for themselves and made life in the Congo a little more tolerable, the 'men only' policy was overturned. This allowed Burton's mind to return to a young lady whom he met while travelling through South Africa. So he promptly returned to visit her – a reunion that resulted in their marriage in May 1918. Years later he recounted, "I went to South Africa one and went back to the Congo two, and I never did a better job in my life!"[53]

---

[51] Burton, W. F. P., *God Working With Them*, Victory Press, London, 1933, p.18.

[52] Ibid, p. 8.

[53] Burton, W. F. P., *The Congo Story*, Tape-recorded message, Circa 1965.

The new Mrs Burton, and other ladies who subsequently joined the mission, adapted quickly, and in a relatively short time they made a great impact, not least with the introduction of maternity care. The local infant mortality rate dropped dramatically, and the mothers were a captive audience for the sharing of the Gospel during their periods of confinement and post-natal care at the mission stations. The missionary women were also free to share the Gospel with the African women in the villages.

Despite the difficulties of international travel in those days, living conditions dictated that it was essential for missionaries to leave the field for a break after a few years – sometimes much sooner – for health reasons. The missionaries often made the journey home to England rather than recuperate nearer to the field, say, in South Africa, thus creating a real opportunity to visit the growing churches back home, share their vision, and enlist not only supporters but also new missionaries. Meeting the needs of the work – both for finance and workers – was a seemingly permanent problem as the mission grew year by year.

As a direct result of one visit to England by Salter, a group of six new missionaries was enlisted and left for Congo in 1920. They included three from Preston, Mr and Mrs Johnstone, who had previously served in the Congo with the Congo Inland Mission, and Mr E (Teddy) Hodgson, who left his promising furniture business in the town to answer the call to the mission field.

Teddy settled in the Kikondja area of the Congo where he worked for some considerable time evangelising the lakeside communities – using the skills of his trade to build boats, which enabled him to minister more effectively to the numerous villages at the water's edge. He was a man's man and his hunting and boat-building skills always ensured a ready audience for his preaching of the Gospel.

The cost to him was very high. He lost his wife in Congo in 1933 and, years later in 1960, Teddy himself paid the ultimate price when he was martyred.[54] Both he and a fellow missionary, Elton Knauf, were murdered at the hands of rebels during the independence uprisings while the missionaries were trying to reach the Christians with aid.

Following Burton's ready change of heart in deciding to enlist women for work in the Congo, it is interesting to note that by the end of the first ten years of the life of the mission, just over half of the missionaries who had left England for the Congo were women.

Amy Entwisle, a young Blackburn spinster and mill-worker, who was one of the original converts and became a founder member of Blackburn Assembly, also became its first missionary. Her brother, Hubert, had been one of Fred Watson's first contacts and had introduced her to the group. Amy felt a call to Africa after attending the annual Easter Pentecostal conventions at Preston – where she heard the exciting accounts of the initial exploits of Burton and Salter in the Congo. A very moving farewell meeting was held in Cort Street and many of the members gathered on Blackburn railway station for a rousing service on the platform as the train pulled out. Amy turned her back on the Lancashire mills and, after language training in France, qualified as a midwife in South Africa before leaving for central Africa in 1926 at the age of 29.

She made the arduous six-week journey to the Congo and found no written local language there. She was handed a list of nouns and verbs – hand written by Willie Burton – and the remainder was learned simply by copying the native tongue. Despite the hard conditions, Amy learned to make bricks so that she could build her own home and a village hospital. The first African baby she delivered she called Ruth, after Fred Watson's baby daughter back home in Blackburn.

Amy was soon established in a village area known as Ngoimani, where she was the only white missionary and worked alone among the Congolese for many years. When, many years later, the Field Conference of the mission

---

[54] Telegram from Kamina, Africa, to J. Salter, 1 December 1960.

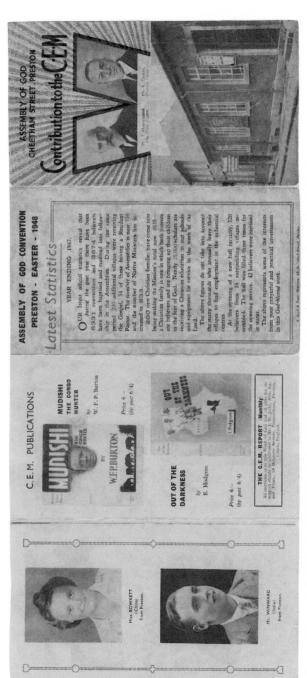

ASSEMBLY OF GOD
CHEETHAM STREET PRESTON

Contribution to the CEM

Mr. T. Myerscough.
The First Pastor.

Mr. R. Coates.
Present Pastor.

ASSEMBLY OF GOD CONVENTION
PRESTON - EASTER - 1948

Latest Statistics

YEAR ENDING 1947.

OUR latest official statistics reveal that during the past year there have been 6,331 conversions and 3,574 believers have been baptised and received into fellowship in the Assemblies. During the same period 200 additional villages were receiving the Gospel, 34 of these having a Resident Pastor. The number of Assemblies is now 749 and the number of Native Ministers has increased to 833.

200 new Christian families have come into being making the Mission's total now 4,619—a Christian family is one in which both parents are believers and are bringing up their children in the fear of God. Nearly 25,000 scholars are receiving a Christian education in our schools and equipment for service in the work of the Lord.

The above figures do not take into account the many thousands who annually leave their villages to find employment in the industrial centres.

At the opening of a new hall recently, 120 believers from 16 surrounding villages assembled. The hall was filled three times for the opening service. 42 believers were baptised in water.

The above represents some of the interests from your prayerful and practical investments in this God-blessed work.

C.E.M. PUBLICATIONS

MUDISHI
THE CONGO
HUNTER
By
W. F. P. Burton

Price 6/–
(by post 6/4)

OUT OF THE
DARKNESS
by
E. Hodgson

Price 6/–
(by post 6/4)

THE C.E.M. REPORT (Monthly)
All enquiries as to the Work of God and all gifts for its support should be addressed to Mr. J. W. Jolly, Hon. Sec. and Treas., 19 Belgrave Avenue, Penwortham, Preston, Lancs., England.

Miss BOWKETT
China
from Preston.

Mr. WINWARD
(India)
from Preston.

Congo Evangelistic Mission (CEM) bulletin, 1948, from Assemblies of God, Cheetham Street, Preston

Frederick Watson – preacher to Mosley Street Primitive Methodist Church, Blackburn.

*Thomas Myerscough – Pentecostal pastor and founder of the Preston
Pentecostal Mission.*

Smith Wigglesworth – pioneering Pentecostal evangelist and inspiration to many.

May 30th 1940.
70 Victor Road
Bradford

Beloved ~~Brother~~ in Christ Jesus
Act–1 must be Fullfilled and
God will not Break His word
then by Faith Place the inclosed
upon you but Read over the 2
Verses of Acts 19th V, 11 & 12 Very
meney times over as Faith
Cimeth by Hearing Gods word
then Repent on all God Shows
you + According to Mark 5th
Verse 36 and Mark 11th
Verses 25.26 then Expect
Perfect deliverence God Bless
you His Servant
        Smith Wigglesworth

I AM THE LORD THAT
HEALETH THEE.
EX. 15/26

An inspiring letter written by
Smith Wigglesworth to a member
of the Blackburn assembly;
inset: a small prayer cloth.
Letter loaned by John Perkins, Blackburn.
Reproduced with permission.

Image of King Street in Blackburn showing the clock tower and market hall

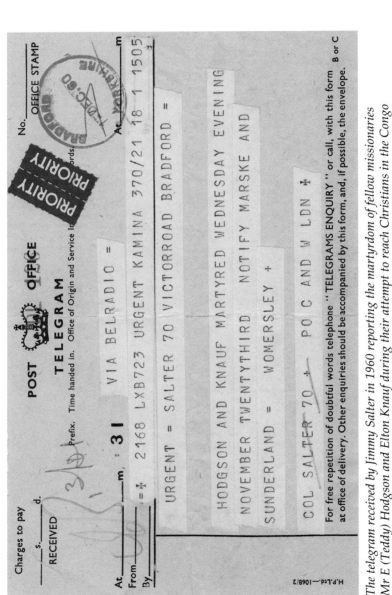

POST OFFICE TELEGRAM

Prefix. Time handed in. Office of Origin and Service Instructions. Words.

Charges to pay

RECEIVED

At.

From

By

No. OFFICE STAMP

At YORKSHIRE

BRADFORD 18 DEC 60

PRIORITY PRIORITY

m. 31

= ⅍ 2168 LXB723 URGENT KAMINA 370/21 18 1 1505

VIA BELRADIO =

URGENT = SALTER 70 VICTORROAD BRADFORD =

HODGSON AND KNAUF MARTYRED WEDNESDAY EVENING

NOVEMBER TWENTYTHIRD NOTIFY MARSKE AND

SUNDERLAND = WOMERSLEY +

COL SALTER 70 + PO C AND W LDN ☩

For free repetition of doubtful words telephone "TELEGRAMS ENQUIRY" or call, with this form B or C at office of delivery. Other enquiries should be accompanied by this form, and, if possible, the envelope.

H.P.Ltd.—1068/2

The telegram received by Jimmy Salter in 1960 reporting the martyrdom of fellow missionaries Mr E (Teddy) Hodgson and Elton Knauf during their attempt to reach Christians in the Congo

Loaned by Central African Missions (formerly CEM). Reproduced with permission.

Blackburn Primitive Methodist First Circuit, 1920: Fred Watson (back row, 3rd from right); Willy Hacking (front row, 2nd from right)

From 'Frederick Watson: A Beloved Pastor', by W Hacking

finally decided to withdraw from Ngoimani, it was a great
personal disappointment to Amy. But the decision stood and
within a short while she retired from missionary service and
left the land of her adoption.

The great missionary meetings at the Preston Easter
Conventions became occasions when new missionaries
shared their vision before leaving for their fields of service. In
1934, the departing missionaries included four local people
leaving for service in the Congo. They were Fred and Isabel
Ramsbottam – who had pioneered a Pentecostal church in
Haslingden, Lancashire; Alfred Brown – a Preston hairdresser
who had more recently "left Cliff College to evangelise in
Newfoundland Canada";[55] and Jim Fowler – a weaver from
Blackburn. Jim was destined to work for many years in an
area of the Congo which, prior to the preaching of the Gospel,
had been a no-go area for many local tribes due to the
cannibalism practised there.

Lawrence and Margaret Livesey, a young married couple
in their early thirties, left Blackburn as missionaries bound for
South India in 1935. They had committed their lives to Christ
in the early 1920s at a cottage meeting held by Amy Entwisle,
and joined the fellowship in Cort Street. Margaret's interest
had first been aroused when she noticed her friend, Amy,
studying French language books propped up on her loom
while they were working together as weavers in a local mill.

Lawrence initially took no interest in Margaret's new faith
but later he too joined the Pentecostal fellowship. They pastored
the Church in Great Harwood for a number of years before
responding to a missionary call. Lawrence was a man of short
build with seemingly boundless energy – revealed not only
in his preaching but also in his readiness to carry out any
necessary manual work. They pursued their missionary call
with considerable energy, for although their departure had
been marked by a special farewell service in the Cort Street
Hall and a 'send off' on Blackburn railway station, their preparation had been neither easy nor rosy.

---

[55] Ramsbottam, F., *African Plenty*, Marshall Pickering, Basingstoke, 1987, p. 31.

During their early days in India, Margaret recorded that "after much discouragement, many disappointments and frustrations, we set sail for the land of our calling."[56] On their arrival, they settled with other missionaries in Pollachi, southern India, and worked in the neighbouring villages. But after a few years they moved to the nearby city of Coimbatore, which became their base for the remainder of the time they were in India. Interestingly, Coimbatore is a textile centre known as 'the Manchester of India'.

The conditions they experienced were appalling, the language extremely difficult, and their problems were clearly exacerbated by the non-arrival of the promised finances from home. Meanwhile, Lawrence built his own bungalow as he studied and preached. The building still stands and its present owner welcomes any visitors and proudly declares that his home was built by an Englishman!

There can be no doubt that many missionaries – however zealous – without Lawrence's resolve and energy, would not have survived such an initiation to the field. Progress was slow and years passed before they saw any converts.

When, during sometime in 1949, the opportunity arose for the purchase of a piece of land suitable for building a church, Lawrence readily sold his bungalow and many of his possessions to buy the property. The present Zion Church stands on that piece of land.

Among all the converts to Christianity during the ministry of the Liveseys, there were two in particular who were to prove pivotal in the life of the Pentecostal church in South India. They were Job Prakasam and Peter Arumainayagam. Today both these men head substantial Pentecostal organisations based in Coimbatore. They are mutually supportive and both see themselves as a "son of Mr and Mrs Livesey". Indeed, in Job's case, his personal relationship with the Liveseys was so strong that they actually fulfilled the Indian custom of parents in finding a wife for their 'son'.[57]

---

56 Livesey, M., *Together with God*, Hulme and Whitehead Ltd., undated, p. 4.
57 Tape-recorded interview with J. Prakasam, Coimbatore, India, March 2001.

Job and Ruth were married in 1938. Today Job is the head of Bethel Fellowship Trust operating from Bethel Church, Coimbatore, and comprises schools, Bible colleges, leper colonies, homes for widows, blind people and children, technical training programmes, and some 300 churches in towns and villages spread across 18 states.

Peter, a young official in agriculture, initially listened to Mr Livesey's preaching simply because he was the first European he had encountered who spoke to Indians in their own tongue. Therefore he decided that their message must be worth hearing, and soon afterwards he sought out Lawrence and became a convert to Christianity.[58] Peter leads the Assemblies of God in Coimbatore, including some 40 churches, children's homes, widows' homes, a Christian literature centre with a wide correspondence ministry, and an outreach across India in disaster-relief work.

Both Peter and Job have the added joy of seeing their sons involved in leadership in the churches. The initial resolve of the Liveseys has been amply rewarded. It is a fitting tribute, albeit one the Liveseys themselves would have doubtless resisted, that a number of the homes, schools and colleges associated with the churches in the Coimbatore area today include the words 'Livesey Memorial' in their official name.

In the late 1920s, a young lady trainee milliner from a professional home became linked with the Blackburn group. Her strict Methodist parents were most concerned about her new religious association, so it was arranged that her younger brother, Alan, would wait outside the Cort Street meeting hall after the services to escort her home in safety. But with the vagaries of Blackburn weather it was not long before he began to wait inside the building, and by 1931 he had committed his life to Christ and soon found himself a committed Pentecostal.

Alan Benson became one of the band of preachers raised up by Fred Watson in Blackburn and, after a period in Bible School,

---

[58] Tape-recorded interview with P. Arumainayagam, Coimbatore, India, March 2001.

he became the pastor of Sharon Tabernacle in Manchester in 1934. But, sometime earlier, Alan had felt a definite call to missionary service and, unable to settle in Manchester, it was not long before he felt compelled to respond to his calling to become a missionary to China. Although he came from a professional family background, he proposed marriage to Violet Mitchell, who came from a lower-class area of the town. A typical characteristic of the early Pentecostal fellowships was the sweeping away of social barriers.

There was no local railway station farewell for Alan. Instead, he hitch-hiked to London – preaching as he went to raise his boat fare – and sailed for China in 1936 at the age of 33. He docked at Shanghai on 30th November of that year.[59] Violet joined him some two years later for a Chinese-style marriage at the British Consulate in Shanghai.

After the necessary language training, they worked in the Kalgan district for some time, and it was there in August 1940 that Alan was summarily arrested by the occupying Japanese military on charges of espionage.[60] The charges were totally without foundation, but the Japanese were wholly unable to accept that any man would leave his secure and comfortable Western way of life and set up home in rural China simply to share his faith. He was held in custody for over seven months, during which time he was repeatedly tortured, both physically and mentally, and ultimately subjected to a farcical trial.

Many people felt that his survival was itself a miracle. He was finally released in March 1941. After a difficult and eventful journey back home, he published his own account of the ordeal he had suffered.[61] Typical of early Pentecostals, he earnestly sought to return to China after the war, but he was unable to obtain a visa.

In 1936, the same year that Alan Benson sailed for China, another young spinster from Blackburn, Hannah Edwards, sailed for the Congo where she served with the CEM for three

---

[59]   *Redemption Tidings*, Volume 13, No. 4, 12 February 1937, p. 8.

[60]   *Daily Mirror*, 30 August 1930, p. 12.

[61]   Benson, A., *Grace Triumphant*, Coulton and Co. Ltd., Nelson, undated.

years. Following her return from the field, she married John Shepherd, the pastor of the Bamber Bridge Fellowship.

The Easter Convention 1938 hosted the farewell of another Lancastrian, Maurice Hugo, who had previously worked for a number of years with Ramsbottams in the church at Haslingden. Following in the footsteps of his friends, he also left Lancashire to join the CEM in the Congo. Maurice served the mission for seventeen years until his sudden death in 1955 whilst itinerating in the homeland.

Alfred Brown completed his first furlough in 1939 and returned as a married man with his new wife, Mary, a Gloucestershire girl who had lived in Preston from her youth. That same Easter the Preston congregation bade farewell to another local boy en-route for Congo, Harold Berry, a young man from the group originally founded by Thomas Mogridge at Lytham some years before.

In 1945 Frank Winward, of farming stock from the village of Brindle, just outside Preston, left the family business to follow his missionary call to China. International travel at the time was difficult – due to the aftermath of war – and the 'normal' route to China was dangerous. But, undaunted, he travelled from Preston to Glasgow, then sailed from Glasgow to North America, traversed North America from east to west, and finally crossed the Pacific to China – no mean feat in those days!

And in that same year, another candidate for the Congo was Mary Jacques, a 27-year-old secretary in the County Offices in Preston, who, although she had originally felt called to Brazil, finally went to the Congo where she served for 38 years.

A small family group from the Cheetham Street Fellowship made their farewells at Easter 1946. They were two sisters: Elsie Billsborough, a 26-year-old teacher, and her older married sister, Ruth Day, also a trained teacher, who, along with Ruth's husband, Walter, and their two young children, were all en route for the CEM in the Belgian Congo.

Elsie's specific task was to be located in Kitwe to undertake the teaching of the children of missionaries on the field. Sadly, Ruth and her family returned home after two years due to personal problems. Elsie returned home in the early 1950s on the death of her father. Their brother, Tom, a Preston elder at the time of their departure, later became the pastor of the Preston Church in 1972.

The Preston Easter Convention missionary day services, which gave a valuable opportunity for returning missionaries to relate first hand their experiences on the field, had also become widely recognised throughout British Assemblies of God as valedictory services for new missionaries to foreign lands, especially for those who had enlisted with the Preston-based Congo Evangelistic Mission. The departing missionaries at the 1948 services not only included the Browns, Amy Entwisle and the Hodgsons – who were returning to the Congo field – but also included the farewell of a local Preston woman, Ruth Bowkett. She was a young nurse who left for China to join her friend Frank Winward who had left some three years before.

A very successful young market gardener of barely 21 years of age from nearby Leyland, Cyril Cross, was fired by the various experiences related by returning missionaries and felt an overpowering call to Tibet. In 1949 he left to pioneer Christian missionary work in that inhospitable country.

Cyril's father, who neither shared nor understood his son's zeal, tried to persuade him to finance someone else to go whilst he remained and enjoyed a comfortable life at home, but Cyril would not be dissuaded. He mastered the very difficult language and became fluent in Tibetan, working in the country for some three years before being compelled to leave due to Communist incursions from China.

But, undaunted by the setback, he remained firmly committed to missions. He returned to England, married Barbara, and together they went to Africa where they served in the Congo for a number of years. Later, after the independence uprisings in the Congo in the early 1960s forced another unplanned departure, they moved on to Nairobi, Kenya, where Cyril founded a Pentecostal Bible Training College that still flourishes today.

The year 1956 saw the departure of Eddie Rowlands for Congo. Eddie had worked in the Preston area for some time before answering the call to Africa, and the following year Clifford Whitham, a Yorkshireman, who had also been living in Preston for a while departed for Africa too. The two men, who had registered as conscientious objectors to military service, had been detailed to do agricultural work in Lancashire for their period of national service, and throughout that time they had fellowshipped at the Cheetham Street Church.

A 25-year-old draughtsman from Zion Chapel in Blackburn, Edwin Holland, sailed for Central Africa aboard the Warwick Castle in October 1957. His destination was not the CEM field but a missionary enterprise among the Kalembelembe tribes of Eastern Congo, an area of missionary work operated by the Overseas Missions Department of British Assemblies of God. The area was inhospitable and, soon after their twins were born, one died in infancy due to the lack of medical help. Edwin, with his Swiss wife, Emily and young family, were evacuated from Congo during the uprising in 1960 and settled in Lytham.

The Easter Convention 1959 was a particularly notable occasion in the life of Preston Assembly in that two of the new missionaries leaving for Congo were Heather and Muriel Atkinson, the two daughters of the pastor of Cheetham Street, George Atkinson. Muriel was a nurse, and Heather was a trained teacher. Heather, shortly after her arrival on the field, married Eddie Rowlands who had left for Congo three years earlier. The wedding ceremony, conducted by Willie Burton, was held on a CEM mission station.

Some months later, when all Western missionaries vacated the field in 1960, at the time of the granting of independence to the Congo, Eddie and the two sisters were evacuated to Salisbury, Rhodesia, in a mission truck driven by Clifford Whitham. While they were there Muriel and Clifford were married.

Typical of the many personal sacrifices which were made for the Gospel's sake, George Atkinson and his wife were unable to attend the wedding of either of their daughters. Muriel and Clifford later settled in the Preston area and pastored the church at Bamber Bridge. Eddie later became a Pentecostal pastor in the South of England.

The list of missionaries sent out from the area cannot be deemed to be complete without recording that there were a number of other missionaries – some perhaps less well-known, but who also readily left the area in response to what they believed to be personal calls of God to go to specific lands – whose travels and accomplishments are not nearly so well documented as those of their contemporaries.

A young man from Leyland, John Parker, spent a few years in Jamaica before returning home in 1949, whereupon he became involved in the oversight of the CEM office in Preston on the death of J Jolly.

Jacqueline Bailley from Blackburn did a sterling work as a missionary in Brazil for many years.

Elisabeth (Lizzie) Hyde, the sister of a Blackburn gents' outfitter, spent some time pioneering churches in Egypt with Mildred Aspden – also from Blackburn – during the 1930s. On their return to England, Lizzie, who was a fiery preacher, served for many years successfully pastoring Assemblies of God churches in Yorkshire.

Walter Cowell, a young man from Preston, and his wife, Bessie, from Lancaster, left England in the 1940s and spent a number of years as missionaries to Jamaica.

Jack Perkins and Fred Sharples from Blackburn went to Holland as missionaries in the late 1930s, and both experienced periods of internment by the Germans soon after the outbreak of war in 1940.

11

Changing Times

The coming of war in 1939 brought many changes and difficulties and the local Pentecostal churches suffered serious
disruptions, as did many organisations in that period. But
sometime during 1942 the Cheetham Street congregation rose
to the challenge by starting a 'Forces Fellowship'. The purpose
was to bring the Gospel to servicemen passing through the
town garrison by offering friendship and a weekly supper at
a specially convened Sunday night after-church rally. The
rallies became a regular feature, and not only did many
young service personnel find Christ in Cheetham Street, but
many lasting friendships were formed at those rallies. A
number of young Christian servicemen and women who were
far from their homes and churches were also encouraged and
strengthened in their faith.[62] The venture, which continued
for some time, was very rewarding and on many Sunday
nights the church was filled to capacity.

The immediate post-war years were no less difficult –
being a time of major readjustment in many areas of national
life – and the Pentecostal churches were no exception.
Servicemen were returning home with a changed perspective
on life, and, although the churches had continued to operate
throughout the war years, it had not been easy. The home-
comings, which had been eagerly anticipated, brought their
own problems. There was pressure for more democracy in the
churches, which, coupled with the problems the missionaries
had faced in travel, communication and finance, resulted in a
period when the Pentecostal zeal of the pre-war years,
although still evident, was somewhat abated.

The two mother churches were settled in their own
buildings and the many branch works were increasingly

---

[62] Tape-recorded interview with Mrs. D. Coates, daughter of J. Jolly, May 2002.

independent. Both churches were well attended, but the
year-on-year growth was not as exciting as it had been
before the war. Conventions had proliferated throughout the
area as new churches had been established, but it was the
main conventions at Preston and Blackburn that played a
major part in keeping the fire burning through these relatively
lean times.

Throughout the war and the immediately subsequent
years, international travel had been very difficult and
missionary furloughs had been virtually impossible. But by
the late 1940s missionaries were again enlisting, and the
Easter Conventions of 1946 and 1948 in particular were
occasions when groups of local folk were again departing for
the foreign mission field or returning after furlough to recount
their experiences.

During the morning service on the last Sunday in January
1952, Richard Coates announced his resignation from the
pastorate of the Preston Assembly. There was a deep sense of
shock in the church, but with the burden of Mrs Coates'
continuing illness, there was also wide understanding of his
desire to devote more of his time to caring for her.

Coates continued to attend the church until some time
before his death in December 1958 at the age of 75. It is a
matter of record that, having accepted Coates' resignation
with genuine regret, the board of elders recommended the
appointment of George Atkinson, one of their number, to the
pastorate. This took place in the same service because the elders
had been informed of Coates' intentions before the service.
Within the space of one morning meeting the pastor had
resigned and a new pastor was in post. George Atkinson, who
was Richard Coates' preferred successor, was a friendly man in
his mid-40s, with a ready smile, and with a more approachable
nature than either of his two predecessors.

The appointment of the pastor from among their own local
board of elders had developed to become a Preston tradition
that continued to operate for many years. They saw the pastor
as a leading elder. Like Myerscough and Coates before him,

Atkinson was a local businessman who, in his case, held a very senior post with the local Electricity Board that he continued to fulfil until his retirement. All three men held the pastoral appointment at Preston in an honorary capacity.

In January 1953, Fred Watson convened his last New Year Convention at Zion Chapel. After a short illness he passed away, after suffering a heart attack on 28th January, at 70 years of age. He had retired from his company post at the age of 60 and publicly asked God for ten more years to devote to the assembly. It would seem that, like Jabez before him, "God granted him what he requested".[63]

The British Pentecostal leadership was well represented at the funeral service at Zion Chapel, which was attended by a near capacity congregation and convened by John Carter, a member of the National Executive of the Assemblies of God. In accordance with his own specific wish, Fred Watson was buried in an unmarked grave in his adopted town of Blackburn. It was the end of an era.

Willie Hacking was the natural choice for successor, having been one of the original members of the founding group. He therefore returned to Blackburn to take over the pastorate, where he was to be the first pastor of either of the two churches to receive a stipend. Willie, who in many respects could be described as Fred Watson's favourite, was totally different from him in almost every respect, although they did share the same reticence to exercise discipline in the assembly.

The older members of the church, many of whom were his contemporaries, always addressed him by his first name, which was unusual for any pastor in those days, and was a major change from the way Fred Watson had always been addressed.

Willie did not find those years in Blackburn an easy time and in 1955 he tendered his resignation from the pastorate – after just over two years in the post. He was aware that Lawrence Livesey was returning from India and, knowing that

63 1 Chronicles 4:10.

the church would be most likely to look to a local man for the succession, stepped down in favour of Lawrence.

Lawrence returned from India in the same year and, on his arrival in England, was invited to assume the pastorate of the Bolton Assembly. Within a few weeks he was also pressed into accepting the pastorate of Blackburn, and so it was that for six months he lived in Blackburn with responsibility for both churches.[64]

Towards the end of 1955 he resigned from the Bolton Assembly to give more time to the Blackburn church, which he pastored until he responded to a call to return to India in October 1960. The Blackburn church not only prospered and grew under his ministry but also experienced a totally new brand of leadership. He was the first pastor at Blackburn to exercise effective discipline, and during his pastorate the first formal membership roll was established.

He was a fiery preacher, thoroughly Pentecostal, and a very practical man. On one occasion, when he became exasperated with the persistent and numerous late arrivals at the services, he instructed that the doors be locked at 10.30 on a particular Sunday morning, and convened the service with a larger congregation outside than inside. But history records that the lesson was effective.

There was, however, another side to his character. When a lady in the congregation who lived alone was distressed because some alterations were urgently needed to widen an outside gateway at her home, she simply asked Livesey to recommend a reliable builder. But she arrived home that evening to find Lawrence was just finishing the job himself!

When Lawrence and Margaret returned to India in 1960 at the specific request of the General Council of Assemblies of God, the Blackburn church felt a real sense of loss. In choosing his successor, they appointed an 'outsider' to the pastorate for the first time.

Throughout the 1950s, both Assemblies were blessed with large numbers of young people within their congregations,

---

[64] Livesey, M., *Together with God*, Hulme and Whitehead Ltd., undated, p. 44.

but changing times meant that these young enthusiasts were seeking to exercise greater influence on the operation and direction of the churches than their seniors seemed able or willing to accept.

Typical of this conflict was the development of the vision for the outreach works in Preston. In the mid-1950s, two branch Sunday schools were opened on the large housing estates on the outskirts of Preston at Ribbleton and Larches. The mother church readily funded the provision of substantial buildings and the two works grew steadily over a number of years. The young men who operated these two outreach works were keen to extend the evangelism on the estates and sought to reach out to the adults as well as to the children. As their vision grew, they asked for permission to hold their own Sunday services in each location in addition to the well-established Sunday School and youth activities.

Sadly, their proposals were seen as a threat to the church rather than as a natural development of the outreach, and their request was refused by the elders, with the result that one or two of the young men concerned left the church. Similarly, the large group of young people in the Blackburn Assembly were not permitted to hold a youth meeting and were not allowed to formally appoint a leader. On one occasion some of the young people were actually rebuked by members of the oversight for attending a Youth for Christ rally in Preston.

Towards the end of the 1950s a series of major changes was proposed for the redevelopment of Preston town centre that was dependent on the Cheetham Street area of the town being scheduled for demolition. The days of Glad Tidings Hall were numbered. Protracted discussions with the council, which were initially frustrating for the church, ultimately resulted in an agreement on compensation, and the fellowship was able to purchase the vacant North Road Methodist Church at the top of Ward Street, just a short distance from Cheetham Street.

After extensive repairs and renovations, the building was formally reopened at Easter 1960 as North Road Pentecostal

Church. The opening ceremony was performed by Willie Burton of CEM, who had also opened the Cheetham Street Hall in 1923. It is interesting to note that by 1960 a number of the Pentecostals in Central Lancashire had come full circle from their Methodist beginnings and the inception of their Pentecostal experiences. They had left Methodism against their better judgement but had arrived at the place where both of the two fellowships were now owners of redundant former Methodist churches that they restored to vibrant places of worship.

It is a credit to Methodism that in each case their representatives gave preferential support to the offer made by the Pentecostals because the building would continue to be used as a place of Christian worship.

12

Recognition

The year 1954 was very significant for spiritual life in Britain, when a national event accelerated the recognition of Pentecostals by the local churches of Lancashire.

Well-known American Evangelist Billy Graham accepted an invitation to conduct a major Gospel crusade in the Harringay Arena in London. These crusade meetings were not primarily Pentecostal but were fundamental and evangelical, and British Pentecostals generally were very supportive.

The crusade was a great success and had a profound effect on churches of all denominations throughout the nation, including the north-west, and it had a particular effect on Pentecostalism generally in Britain.

British Pentecostals had, for decades, been ostracised by the Church at large; but the situation in America was rather different in the 1950s. In the crusade planning meetings, members representing the Billy Graham team had apparently indicated their willingness for Pentecostals to be recognised as acceptable participants. Although there had already been some evidence of a slight thaw in the attitudes of other churches towards Pentecostals, formal acceptance into such a significant event was a major step forward on the road to recognition.

There was immediate local evidence of the improved relationship produced by the crusade when a number of the evangelical churches of Blackburn organised a special crusade train from the town to London. For the first time, the members of the local Pentecostal Assembly found themselves working together with the Anglicans, Methodists and Baptists of the town and travelling to London together in a united act of fellowship, publicity and cooperation.

Bridges were being built, and the move had commenced on the road towards recognition of Pentecostals by the established churches. This was not simply a qualified recognition of the local Pentecostal Assemblies as a part of the Christian scene but, much more importantly, acceptance of the place of Pentecostalism generally in the Christian faith. Despite the improved relationship, however, neither side was to find the road an easy one.

Whilst the founding fathers had initially sought to take Pentecostalism back into the established churches rather than form their own congregations, their subsequent rejection and the many years of isolation made the journey down the road to reconciliation just as difficult for the Pentecostals as for the established churches.

Some Pentecostals had grown to feel that, because they had an experience that the other churches did not and would not share, that somehow they had therefore become spiritually superior. When a number of local Pentecostals began to enjoy fellowship and share in Gospel outreach with other local churches in the 1950s, they were openly rebuked and warned of backsliding by their leaders. Ironically, whilst in the early days the founders had genuinely sought opportunity to take Pentecost into the churches, when that same opportunity was finally presented to their successors, they were resistant.

There was a suggestion that, at least in some respects, when the opportunity for reconciliation arose, it was the established churches that were being rejected by the Pentecostals. The Pentecostals faced the real danger of adopting the insular mentality of that now rather famous headline in a national newspaper – 'Europe Cut Off' – on the occasion of a 'pea soup' fog that remained all day over the English Channel.

The early Pentecostals neither sought nor desired any form of public recognition. Indeed, initially, they tended to view any form of publicity or links with authority as decadent. There was therefore some surprise among their ranks when a fitting tribute was indirectly paid to the work of the group of Pentecostal missionaries from Lancashire, in the form of the official recognition that was ultimately awarded to one of their number.

Amy Entwisle's brother, Hubert, had emigrated from Britain to America as a young man but had kept in close touch with his sister and maintained his Blackburn links over the years. Hubert had been one of the original Blackburn group. Having become involved in local government in America, he felt very strongly that Amy's missionary service justified some formal recognition. So he contacted the Belgian Government and, in due course, Amy was formally awarded their official medal for her long missionary service in the Belgian Congo. It is appropriate to note also that, a number of years later, Hubert made representations to the British authorities, and in the 1980s Amy was additionally awarded the MBE in recognition of her missionary work in the Congo.[65]

---

[65] *Blackburn Evening Telegraph*, date unknown.

13

The Legacy

In concluding this study, it is beneficial to review our findings in order to understand more fully the quality and extent of the spiritual legacy that accrued over the first 50 years, and which evolved largely as a result of the vision and ministry of the two pioneers – Watson and Myerscough.

The initial formation and gradual establishment of the two, strong Pentecostal churches at Blackburn and Preston, provided a sound base for the further spread of Pentecostalism throughout the area. This, coupled with the development of the Preston Bible School in the early years, produced many future Pentecostal leaders such as George Jeffreys and Willie Burton, who were sent out into a wide field of ministry.

Both of the founding fathers were deeply involved in the formation of the Assemblies of God in Great Britain in 1924, and served on its Executive Presbytery for a number of the formative years. The Assemblies of God was destined to become the largest group of mainline Pentecostal churches in Great Britain.

From the two mother churches, at least 13 satellite churches were founded in towns and villages scattered around the immediate area of Lancashire, together with two branch works on large housing estates in Preston, and a branch Sunday School on the Shadsworth estate in Blackburn.

Young men and women, often relatively new converts, many with no spiritual background whatsoever, were trained and sent out, not only into pastoral ministry in the satellite churches, but also into the wider British Pentecostal ministry. In all, a total of some 30 pastors were sent out, of whom three settled in North America and two were interned in Holland by Nazi Germany during World War II.

Over the years there were, in addition to the pastors,

a very significant number of local young men who were engaged in an itinerant lay ministry in Pentecostal churches around Lancashire and further afield.

A total of at least 38 missionaries went out from the central Lancashire Pentecostal churches over the period, of whom at least six had previously held pastorates in the homeland. They took the Gospel and 'Pentecostal fire' to India, Tibet, Brazil, Egypt, Jamaica, China and Africa. One was interned and tortured by the Japanese in China, and rebels in Africa martyred another. Twenty-two of the missionaries served in Central Africa with the Congo Evangelistic Mission that was founded in the early 1920s by the first two Pentecostal missionaries from Preston – Burton and Salter. The mission, now known as the Central African Mission, continues to operate from its base in Preston.

In many instances there is no identifiable record of what was actually achieved by the Pentecostal missionaries from Lancashire. Perhaps only eternity will reveal the fruit of their labours. However, the records of the CEM alone show that by 1960, just before the field was vacated due to the post-independence uprising, there were 75 foreign missionaries associated with the work, 14 mission stations, over 1,000 churches and 43,000 Pentecostal African believers.

During the 1940s, a rather unexpected series of events sparked further development of Pentecostalism in the Blackburn area – when two new congregations were established in the town, both of which later became affiliated with national Pentecostal Fellowships.

As mentioned earlier in this book, the Bethel Evangelical Church, founded immediately after the Jeffreys crusade in the town, had acquired the large redundant Congregational Church at the top of Montague Street in the late 1930s. The purchase had been facilitated by money borrowed from a local Christian businessman. However, within a few years, he requested the return of the loan and the church had to be sold.

Whilst the church was seeking new premises they suffered a split in their ranks. Two new groups were formed –

one group moved into a hall in Randal Street and the other purchased premises on Northgate.

The Randal Street group became Pentecostal and joined the Apostolic Church. The Randal Street Apostolic Church as a smaller church developed a local link with the larger Zion Chapel Assemblies of God, and the two churches enjoyed a period of Pentecostal inter-church fellowship for a number of years.

The Northgate group retained their links with Bethel for a while, but in the late 1940s they too became Pentecostal, joined the Elim Alliance, and appointed Stanley Beresford of Westhoughton Assemblies of God as their pastor.

In the later years of the period covered by this book, there were signs of a change in the general attitude of a number of the local established denominations towards Pentecostalism. This qualified acceptance that Pentecostals enjoyed was to become an important factor in the spiritual realignment within many of the established churches in subsequent years. It is noteworthy, for example, that F F Bruce, when discussing a proposed visit to North America in 1968 with a fellow elder of the local Brethren Church, records having said: "I shall probably come back speaking with tongues".[66]

By 1960 there were initial signs that Pentecostalism was beginning to operate within the historic churches of Lancashire and, in doing so, it had not only come full circle in 50 years, but had also begun to realise the original intentions of the early Pentecostal pioneers.

---

[66]   Bruce, F. F., *In Retrospect*, Marshall Pickering, London, 1993, p. 242.

14

Review and Reflections

Notwithstanding the relatively impressive growth which local Pentecostalism accomplished, particularly in its early years, when compared with other Christian churches in the Lancashire area, there are a number of aspects of their *modus operandi* which warrant examination and could possibly have produced even greater results had they been handled differently.

Firstly, in the area of leadership, it is clear that the successors of the two founding fathers did not see the same rate of growth as their mentors, despite the fact that in each case they had, as members of the group, lived and ministered alongside the founders over a number of years before stepping into their shoes.

Whilst Myerscough did establish a Bible School in Preston and training for ministry generally was clearly a part of the developed programme, there is nevertheless little evidence of any real attention to specific preparations for succession by either leader. Both men died in office and therefore were not available for counsel at the time of succession – a period which both churches found to be very difficult. This was made more difficult in each case by the deep sense of loss at the founder's death.

The lack of effective succession in leadership was a generally weak area in the 20th century British Pentecostalism in the early years. In their zeal, Pentecostals jettisoned many of the established practices of the historic denominations that they often perceived to be decadent. In doing so, they discarded some practices that may have been beneficial, typical of which were systems of training for ministry and succession. It must be said in their defence that they were convinced that they were living in the 'Last Days' and were eagerly anticipat-

ing the return of Jesus Christ to earth for his Church.[67] Therefore their tendency was to place less emphasis than may have
been appropriate on earthly continuation. The adoption of
some form of training similar to the Anglican system of
curacy may well have been advantageous to them.

Secondly, an observer may question their general
deployment of men and women in ministry. From these two
churches and their satellites there went out a relatively large
group of missionaries, a number of whom were very high
achievers in their chosen ministry, and literally hundreds of
churches were established in various parts of the world as a
result of their spiritual convictions and pioneering spirit.
There is a valid argument that some of their best people went
to the foreign field, which begs this question: Would we have
witnessed a very different outcome in the homeland if they
had remained in Lancashire and applied their natural abilities
and spiritual anointing locally?

Whilst we must not fail to take into account the important
fact that those who left for the mission field did so in response
to what they saw as the call of God, there is equally no doubt
that they would have made a considerable impact at home.
Men like Burton, Hodgson and Livesey, for example, were all
strong individualists with an independent spirit whose
successes abroad were heartily applauded by the home
churches. But perhaps they may have found a less ready
acceptance had they remained in the homeland and demonstrated those same qualities in the somewhat closer confines
of the developing local Pentecostal church community. Is
it possible that, although the churches had been established
by godly men of strong character, those same men would
have found themselves unable, or at least found it difficult,
to accommodate into their ranks as leaders a new wave of
younger men with similar qualities to their own? Is it also
possible that many of the members themselves would have
had more difficulty respecting one of their contemporaries
than an older man?

---

[67]   1 Thessalonians 4:16 - 18.

Thirdly, their employment of finances is of interest. The early Pentecostals gave liberally to the Church. On one occasion, whilst itinerating during a furlough from Africa in 1939, Jim Fowler received an offering of £62.23 while visiting his home Assembly at Blackburn to report on his missionary work. In a later letter to Jimmy Salter he records that the offering "came much above the expectations of Brother Myerscough or ourselves". This was a significant amount of money in 1939, particularly from a mid-week congregation that was predominantly working-class.

The missionary offerings received at the annual conventions over the years were also significant sums, regularly amounting to thousands of pounds on Easter Monday. Yet year-by-year all the money received was dispensed to foreign missions with the exception of basic outgoings. The record shows, however, that the relatively modest investment in the two church properties in Blackburn and Preston proved to be extremely beneficial when, in later years, the local authority responsible for redevelopment purchased both churches' buildings. The total cost of the two buildings together was little more than one thousand pounds. The funds received in compensation financed the acquisition of alternative buildings.

Despite some very sacrificial giving in the early years, the Pentecostals have often found in subsequent years that their vision was limited by lack of funds, whilst many other religious organisations were able to survive on investments which, having ameliorated over time, augmented the regular income from their congregations.

It is interesting that, whilst both founders were businessmen, there is no record of any proposals to invest even a part of the money received in town centre properties. Such investments would have not only provided regular income for the work but also realised ultimately a very substantial asset value. However, it must be recognised that their spiritual vision was so intense that, at that time, they would have regarded any investment for future financial benefit as worldly.

Fourthly, we note that if we examine the growth trends of the Lancashire Pentecostal churches over the 50 years, the rate of growth was greatest in the early years. For example, with the exception of Larches and Ribbleton in Preston, all the other branch churches were opened within the first 30 years. Whilst the churches generally remained healthy and vibrant, they passed through a period when there was considerably less emphasis on outreach, which had been a primary quality of the pioneering spirit of the formative years. Doubtless World War II was a significant factor, but there must also be spiritual factors that contributed to the general scenario.

It is a sad indictment on human nature that all revivals 'settle down'. Sadly, the Lancashire Pentecostals were no exception. The ardent fervour of the early days was certainly not lost, but neither was it maintained either in themselves or their converts. Perhaps partly as a result of the continuing rejection they suffered, the thrills and excitement of Pentecostalism became matters for enjoyment within the fellowship rather than proclamation outside it.

It is noteworthy that, as early as 1934, Edward Jeffreys, who saw some dramatic responses in his nationwide crusades of the '30s, wrote: "I have no patience with people who say they are baptised in the Holy Spirit, and no passion for souls confined to their own mission halls and drawing rooms, shaking and making hideous noises. Some people's conception of Pentecost is very selfish."[68] There may be those who would perhaps make the same comment about some of the more recent Pentecostal events of the 1990s.

Finally, to ascertain the impact and effect of Pentecostalism, we do well to compare the initial vision of the pioneers with the resultant situation at the end the period covered by our study.

We have established earlier that the founding fathers of the two churches did not initially set out with any intention of forming separate Pentecostal churches but were compelled to

---

[68] *The Bethel Full Gospel Messenger*, Volume 5, Number 12, December 1931, p. 187.

do so following the rejection of Pentecostalism by the historic churches. During the period that we have examined, the initial attitude of rejection gradually became one of tolerance, and subsequently tolerance gave way to a form of cautious acceptance. By the end of the same period, many statistics of religion were showing that Pentecostals tended to be more committed, and their churches were growing faster, than most other Christian groups. There was also confirmation that the Pentecostal experience was beginning to find qualified acceptance within the historic churches.

In seeking to define the impact and effect of Pentecostalism in central Lancashire, we must consider whether or not there is a possibility that, when the historic churches were unable to accept an outpouring of the Holy Spirit, God raised up a group of people in Lancashire and in many other places who, under some divine programme, formed groups of Pentecostal churches which preserved this specific area of essential Christian teaching. A biblical teaching, which had come full circle by the end of the period we are studying, had begun to find acceptance in the historic churches. Such a possibility suggests that these men and women had fulfilled the purpose of God and fulfilled it so effectively that, in subsequent years, the Pentecostal experience was increasingly present in many churches within the historic denominations.[69] There can be no doubt that both Myerscough and Watson would have seen the ultimate acceptance of Pentecostalism by the historic churches as a fulfilment of their initial vision.

Mainline Pentecostals generally would readily accept that Pentecostalism is an experience and not a denomination. Perhaps it could be argued therefore that there is a sense in which the Pentecostal churches both locally and nationally had come full circle and effectively completed the task which they were originally prevented from accomplishing, and had, albeit indirectly, served their primary purpose which was to bring the Church into a Pentecostal experience. That premise begs a further question on the future of Pentecostal

---

[69] *World Almanac and Book of Facts*, Pan Books Ltd., London, 1993, p. 537.

churches generally, which does not have a simple answer and it is not the object of this book to attempt to provide one.

Bibliography

Allen, D., *The Unfailing Stream*, Tonbridge, Sovereign, 1994.

Benson, A., *Grace Triumphant*, Coulton and Co. Ltd., Nelson, undated.

Bruce, F. F., *In Retrospect*, Marshall Pickering, London, 1993.

Burton, A., *The Rise and Fall of King Cotton*, British Broadcasting Corporation, London, 1984.

Burton, W. F. P., *God Working With Them*, Victory Press, London, 1933.

Cox, H., *Fire from Heaven*, London, Cassell, 1996.

Gee, D., *The Pentecostal Movement*, Victory Press, London, 1941.

Gee, D., *These Men I Knew*, Assemblies of God Publishing House, Nottingham, 1980.

Hacking, W., *Frederick Watson*, R. Seed & Sons, Preston, 1953.

Hunt, D., *A History of Preston,* Carnegie Publishing Ltd., Preston, 1992.

Livesey, M., *Together with God*, Hulme and Whitehead Ltd., undated.

Ramsbottam, F., *African Plenty*, Marshall Pickering, Basingstoke, 1987.

Timmins, G., Blackburn, *A Pictorial History*, Phillimore & Co. Ltd., Chichester, 1993.

Timmins, G., Preston, *A Pictorial History*, Phillimore & Co. Ltd., Chichester, 1992.

Whittaker, C., *Seven Pentecostal Pioneers*, Marshall Morgan & Scott, Basingstoke, 1983.

Woodruff, W., *The Road to Nab End*, Abacus, London, 2002.

Journals, Newspapers, Tape-recorded interviews, etc.,

Telegram from Kamina, Africa to J. Salter, 1 December 1960.

Burton, W. F. P., *The Congo Story*, Tape-recorded message, Circa 1965.

The Bethel Full Gospel Messenger, Volume 5, Number 12, December 1931.

The Bethel Pictorial Guide, 1928 - 1938.

Blackburn Evening Telegraph, date unknown.

Daily Mirror, 30 August 1930.

Northern Daily Telegraph, 24 November 1931.

Preston Chronicle, Preston Riots, Black Saturday, 13 August 1842.

Redemption Tidings, Volume 8, No. 4, April 1932.

Redemption Tidings, Volume 13, No. 4, 12 February 1937.

Tape-recorded interview with P. Arumainayagam, Coimbatore, India, March 2001.

Tape-recorded interview with T. Billsborough, Pastor of North Road Church, 1971 - 1979, June 2002.

Tape-recorded interview with Mrs. D. Coates, daughter of J. Jolly, May 2002.

Tape-recorded interview with Mrs. L. Norcross, May 2002.

Tape-recorded interview with W. Hacking, May 2001.

Tape-recorded interview with J. Prakasam, Coimbatore, India, March 2001.

World Almanac and Book of Facts, Pan Books Ltd., London, 1993.

<u>Cornerstone Church.</u>

Lord's Stile Lane. Bromley Cross.

Bolton.   **BL7 9JL**

Phone 01204 597311

Sunday Morning Worship

11.00 a.m.